Current Issues in Irish Health Management

A Comparative Review

Tim O'Sullivan
Michelle Butler

IPA
INSTITUTE OF PUBLIC
ADMINISTRATION

First published in 2002
by the Institute of Public Administration
57-61 Lansdowne Road
Dublin 4
Ireland

www.ipa.ie

ISBN 1 902448 68 5

British Library Cataloguing in Publication Data
A catalogue record for this book is available from the British
Library

Cover design by Creative Inputs
Typeset by the Institute of Public Administration
Printed by Johnswood Press

Contents

Foreword

A great deal has been written on the health care system in Ireland in recent years and this book builds on the work of many researchers on the health care system in Ireland and elsewhere. Our thanks are due first therefore to the researchers, health care professionals and managers whose writings have informed our analysis and contributed to our thinking on comparative health care.

Sincere thanks are due to Philip Berman, Director of the European Health Management Association (EHMA), for generously sharing insights drawn from his in-depth knowledge of comparative issues, for his advice on approaches to comparative health care and for his valuable comments.

We are particularly indebted to Tony McNamara of the IPA, for his encouragement of this project from its inception and for his skilled editorial work on successive drafts of the book. Our work was greatly enhanced by his first-rate editorial input.

A special thanks too to Carolyn Gormley for her skilled and professional contribution to the preparation and presentation of the book.

The introductory and concluding chapters were jointly written. Michelle Butler wrote the chapters on health gain, service planning, developing performance measurement and quality management in healthcare (chapters 4, 6, 7 and 8). Tim O'Sullivan wrote the chapters on the benefits of comparative healthcare, a selective guide to the literature, the public-private mix and the voluntary sector in the health services (chapters 2, 3, 5 and 9).

Responsibility for the content of the book and for any deficiencies which remain rests with the authors.

Michelle Butler
Tim O'Sullivan
February 2002

Chapter 1
Introduction

Health and healthcare have for many years been at, or close to, the top of the political and media agenda in Ireland. Issues as diverse as hospital waiting lists, spending trends, inequities between public and private patients, contaminated blood, consultants' contracts, recruitment and retention of key personnel and the achievement of improvements in health status (to take just a few examples) are seldom far from the headlines – or from public controversy.

In the last decade or so, since the publication of *Health – the Wider Dimensions* in 1986, *The Report of the Commission on Health Funding* in 1989 and *Shaping a Healthier Future* in 1994, the achievement of health care reform has been a major theme of Irish policymakers. These publications and strategies have also strongly influenced the shape of that reform. At the time of publication (2001), a new strategy, *Quality and Fairness, A Health System for You*, has just been launched by the Department of Health and Children and will shape the future direction of the Irish health services for the coming years.

An increasing feature of health policy discussion in Ireland is a strong emphasis on comparative review. The Commission on Health Funding reflected, for example, on funding trends in the social insurance systems of continental Europe. In developing policy on private health insurance, the 1999 white paper on that topic took account of insurance trends elsewhere. The 1994 and 2001 *Health Strategies* compared basic Irish statistics on life expectancy and mortality to those in other EU countries. In official Irish publications, Irish statistics are constantly compared with those from other OECD or EU countries.

Nevertheless, it is generally not part of the brief of official publications to provide a detailed reflection on comparative trends or on key questions such as: What is happening elsewhere? What can be learned from trends elsewhere? How are current issues in Irish health management illuminated by analysis of international trends?

The brief of this book, by contrast, is to reflect on these precise questions. It begins with two context-setting chapters on comparative study and on comparative literature. It then focuses on some key themes and issues in current management and policy in Ireland: the public-private mix, health gain, service planning, performance measurement, quality management and the role of the voluntary sector.

Recent discussion in Ireland and elsewhere on comparative health care has been stimulated by the publication in 2000 of the *World Health Report* of the WHO. This document identifies four vital functions of health systems – (service provision, resource generation, financing and stewardship) and three goals or objectives which are closely related to the four vital functions (health improvement, responsiveness to the expectations of consumers and fairness in financial contribution).

Many of the themes and issues which we consider in the Irish context are closely linked to the broad health care goals and functions identified by the WHO in 2000. To take just two examples, there are close links between the WHO goal of health improvement and our chapter on health gain (Chapter 4); or between the WHO functions of financing and stewardship and our chapters on the public-private mix (Chapter 5) and on statutory and voluntary relationships (Chapter 9). Important underlying issues here, on which views may differ, are the appropriate role of the state in the funding and provision of health care and the implications of a commitment to equity in health care. Is it more equitable, for example, for the state to fund free health care for all citizens or to focus instead on funding care for those who are more needy?

In this book, topics related to the goals and functions of health systems are explored from the perspective of current Irish debates and issues. We seek to draw lessons for Ireland from reflection on the themes covered in the various chapters. The methodology adopted is to report on current issues and developments in Ireland and then to consider possible lessons for this country on the basis of an examination of trends in other developed countries.

It is necessary first, however, to place the Irish healthcare system in a general context and to report on some key developments in Irish healthcare. The purpose of the remainder of this chapter is to identify the key issues facing the Irish health services at the beginning of the twenty-first century and to outline some of the thinking behind current reforms, in order to set the context for the range of issues covered in subsequent chapters.

OVERVIEW OF THE IRISH HEALTH SYSTEM

The Irish health care system is a largely tax-funded one which incorporates a significant public-private mix. An OECD review in 1997 commented that 'the Irish health service is based on a mixture of public and private care which has resulted in good provision of healthcare at relatively low cost to the taxpayer' (p.150). Since 1991, there has been universal coverage for hospital services but only 30 per cent of the population, who have category 1 eligibility, are exempt from the payment of fees for general practitioner care (General Medical Services (Payments) Board, 2001). Although there is universal coverage for hospital services, around 42 per cent of the population has private health insurance to cover the costs of private hospital care; those with private health insurance enjoy tax relief on their premiums. Private funding amounts to 22 per cent of total funding. (Department of Health and Children, 2001a)

The OECD (1997) argued that the mix of public and private care in Ireland is similar in some respects to that found in some US states and Canadian provinces, in Australia and to a certain extent the Netherlands. However, it identified some essential differences in the Irish context: the role of the VHI as a statutory non-profit organisation; the requirement for two-thirds of patients (Category II) to pay a fee to cover marginal costs at the point of delivery for first-level medical care, which serves to limit demand; the fact that both public and private services can be secured from the same provider (OECD, 1997).

Since 1971, Ireland has been divided into eight regions for the purposes of health care management. The 1970 Health Act, which established the regional health boards, also established Comhairle na nOspidéal (the Hospitals' Council), which regulates hospital consultant appointments and advises the minister on acute hospital services. Other major players in the Irish health services include the public voluntary hospitals and a number of large intellectual disability (mental handicap) agencies, which are mostly funded by the state and enjoy significant independence. They have traditionally been directly funded by the Department of Health and Children but will in future be funded by regional authorities. In March 2000, the Eastern region, which includes Dublin, Kildare and Wicklow, was sub-divided into three area health boards which are under the control of a new Eastern Regional Health Authority (ERHA). All agencies in the region, both statutory and voluntary, receive their funding from the same source: the ERHA.

O'Hara (1998) provides a comprehensive overview of the current structure of the Irish health system. She outlines the roles of the legislature and government, and of the Minister and Secretary General of the Department of Health and Children and of the department itself. Beyond the level of the Department of Health and Children, O'Hara identified five types of bodies with responsibility for the provision of health services:

- *Health boards* – the ERHA and the regional health boards around the country serve populations of between 200,000 and 1.3 million people and each has its own chief executive officer. Management boards are made up of elected local representatives, ministerial nominees and employee representatives.
- *Voluntary hospitals and other voluntary agencies*
- *Specialist bodies* – established under specific acts, such as the Irish Medicines Board and Comhairle na nOspidéal.
- *Bodies established under the Health (Corporate Bodies) Act, 1961*. This Act enables the Minister for Health and Children to establish advisory and service agencies without the need for a separate Act each time.
- *Registration bodies* – agencies established under specific Acts to regulate the main professions.

Health spending has been increasing significantly in recent years after the cutbacks of the 1980s. The OECD (1997) reports that while total health spending (both public and private) as a proportion of gross national product (GNP) rose in most countries over the preceding years, Ireland experienced a drop in the share of its GNP devoted to health care. As a result, in the period from 1980 to 1993, spending in Ireland as a proportion of GNP went from being one of the highest in OECD countries to being one of the lowest. This is partly related to very rapid growth in the Irish economy in the 1990s: health spending rose but not at the same rate as economic growth generally. In real terms, Irish spending on health increased significantly in the 1990s and particularly in recent years. Gross public spending on health will increase from just under £4.3 billion in 2000 to about £5.3 billion in 2001. The 2001 *Health Strategy* estimated that Ireland's health spending per capita in 2001 was 2,109 US $ and thus slightly above the average in the rest of the EU (2097 $). The equivalent figures for 1990 were 756 $ (Ireland) and 1,223$ (Rest of the EU) (Department of Health and Children, 2001a, p. 45)

The future of the health services has been the subject of much debate and analysis. The *Health Strategy* document of 1994 set out the major direction for the health services in the 1990s. This was followed in 2001, with the second health strategy: *Quality and Fairness, A Health System for You.*

Key policy challenges include ensuring that accessible, timely and high-quality health services are available to Irish citizens; that these services are adequately staffed by skilled and motivated personnel; and that public patients enjoy a similar level of access to the health services as private patients. Along with the concepts of equity, quality and accountability promoted in the 1994 strategy, the 2001 strategy promulgates the concept of people-centred health and social services. This alone will require significant reform to enable health care to be delivered in such a way that it is responsive to individual needs, 'is planned and delivered in a co-ordinated way', and 'helps individuals to participate in decision making to improve their health' (Department of Health and Children, 2001a, p.18).

The principle of equity is promoted as central to policy development in the new strategy, both in terms of access to services and in terms of addressing differences in health status between groups within Irish society. Thus the concept of equity embraces health and social gain. Quality, and the development of a quality culture throughout the health system, is another central theme in the strategy, which seeks to build on the work carried out since 1994 by developing a more co-ordinated and comprehensive approach. The new strategy also seeks to 'underpin' financial, organisational and professional accountability with a focus on improving planning and evaluation, the development of performance measurement systems, strengthening and clarifying accountability, the development of evidence-based practice and clarifying the rights and expectations of patients.

A CHRONOLOGY OF RECENT REFORMS

O'Hara (1998) suggests that the government's consultative statement – *Health: the Wider Dimensions* (Department of Health, 1986) – was the first attempt at setting a direction for health services and at planning services in relation to meeting health-related targets. This was followed in 1987 with the establishment of the Commission on Health Funding, which identified several weaknesses in the organisation of health services. While the Commission on Health Funding was established primarily to examine the financing of health services, one of its key findings was that

> ... the solution to the problem facing the Irish health services does not lie primarily in the system of funding but rather in the way that services are planned, organised and delivered (Report of the Commission for Health Funding, 1989, p.15).

This review was then followed up in 1994 with the publication by the Department of Health of *Shaping a Healthier Future*, which came to be known widely as the *Health Strategy*. The main theme was to re-orientate the system towards improving the effectiveness of health and personal social services. Accordingly, the strategy promotes: the need to focus prevention, treatment and care services more clearly on improvements in health status and the quality of life – with increased emphasis on the appropriateness of care; the provision of more decision making and accountability at regional level through changes in management and organisational structures, allied to better performance measurement; greater sensitivity to the rights of consumers, responsiveness of services, equity and quality of service – and enabling providers to move in this direction.

Amongst the weaknesses which the strategy identified in the system were: insufficient attention to tackling the causes of premature mortality; long waiting times for services; inadequate linkages between complementary services; community-based services which are not yet well enough developed to substitute for institutional care; and management and organisational structures in need of updating.

Following up on this strategy, Dixon and Baker (1996) were commissioned by the department to conduct a thorough review of management development needs across the system and to assist in the preparation of a ten-year management development strategy. This strategy was published at the end of 1996 and led to the establishment of the Office for Health Management in 1997.

In 1998, the Department of Health and Children published its strategy statement *Working for Health and Well-Being*. This outlines the department's mission and high level and divisional objectives within the current environment of the health sector and its role with its 'partners' in planning and delivering health services. Key themes in the department's mission are: partnership and co-operation; protecting, promoting and restoring health and well-being; and effective planning, management and delivery of health and personal social services to achieve measurable health and social gain and provide the optimum return on resources. These themes are then reflected in the high level objectives, which emphasise partnership, strategic development, accountability, quality and effectiveness and a customer service ethos.

A series of strategy documents has been published relating to various aspects of health service development identified in *Shaping a Healthier Future*. These include the National Cancer Strategy (1996); *Building Healthier Hearts: The Report of the Cardiovascular Health Strategy Group* (1999); and *The National Health Promotion Strategy* (1995 and 2000). There have also been several policy documents and action plans relating to the implementation of programmes to meet targets set out in the health strategy. The new *Health Strategy* (2001) outlines four goals for the health system: better health for everyone; fair access; responsive and appropriate care delivery; and high performance. Several objectives are identified for each of these goals, which are outlined in an action plan to be achieved over the next ten years, along with specific targets, dates and responsibilities

Along with these changes in thinking, strategy and policy, several structural reforms were implemented in line with the decisions of the 1994 *Health Strategy*. The reforms aimed to enhance accountability, coordination of services and cost containment and promote, to a limited extent, market approaches or terminology. This can be seen in the increased use of contracting and service agreement terminology in the health services and in the distinction drawn between the commissioning and providing of services – even in the context of public funding and provision of services. Distinctions are being made (particularly in the Eastern region) between the body funding services (the regional authority) and the bodies providing services (for example, a state-run hospital, which is publicly funded and owned, on the one hand, and on the other a public voluntary hospital, which is largely publicly funded but generally owned by a charity or religious order).

In 1996, accountability legislation – The Health (Amendment) (No. 3) Act – was introduced with three main objectives: to strengthen and improve the arrangements governing financial accountability and expenditure procedures in health boards; to clarify the respective roles of the members of health boards and their chief executive officers; and to begin the process of removing the Department of Health from detailed involvement in operational matters. The preparation of detailed service plans by health agencies (setting out in detail their planned activities and spending for the year ahead) is a key part of this legislative reform and is now one of the main management tasks of each health agency. Such plans are submitted for approval to the Department of Health and Children. The new health strategy aims to further develop the service planning process, with a particular focus on developing the monitoring and evaluation of objectives outlined in service plans.

Also, in line with the 1994 strategy, funding of the large voluntary agencies has been transferred from the Department of Health and Children to the regional health authorities. Complex issues arose in particular in the Eastern region (including Dublin), where many of the voluntary hospitals and large voluntary mental handicap agencies are situated.

In November 1998, the final report of a task force on the Eastern region and the proposed legislation for the organisation of services in the region were published. In May 1999 the Health (ERHA) Act was passed. The Act followed the recommendations of the task force and provided for three area health boards within the region. The ERHA (which came into operation in March 2000) now funds all statutory and voluntary services in the region. It will focus on the strategic planning of services in the region and on the commissioning of those services from both the statutory and voluntary sectors.

One of the changes envisaged by the 1994 strategy was that the large intellectual disability/mental handicap agencies, which provide most mental handicap services in Ireland and were traditionally funded directly by the Department of Health, would also be funded from now on by their regional health authorities. The report of a working group in 1997 on the implementation of the *Health Strategy* in relation to persons with a mental handicap – *Enhancing the Partnership* – recommended the establishment of service agreements, an agreed planning framework and the development of high quality data through a national mental handicap database. This document highlighted some other core principles which should underpin service agreements, including the operation of such agreements for a number of years, with provision for annual allocations. It also provided for independent arbitration where problems have not been resolved by the health board and the voluntary agency.

In 1998, responsibility for funding the large mental handicap providers in the Southern and Mid-Western Health Boards passed from the Department of Health and Children to the local health boards in accordance with the principles and procedures set out in *Enhancing the Partnership*. The other health boards later followed suit.

Significant structural changes are also likely to fall out of the new health strategy. Thus the proposed new primary care teams and networks are designed to achieve greater health care integration and more appropriate use of the health services. The proposed actions for primary care are outlined in a supplement to the strategy: *Primary Care: A New Direction* (Department of Health and Children, 2001b). In addition, the number, structure and organisation of health boards and agencies is to be subject to an independent review. The new strategy also proposes the establishment of a number of new independent statutory bodies, such as the Health Information and Quality Authority and the National Hospitals Agency. Also proposed in terms of structural reforms, is the establishment of a new Division of Population Health in the Department of Health and Children, which will work closely with new population health functions to be developed in health boards.

CURRENT POLICY CHALLENGES

Three key themes or challenges can be identified from major recent national policy documents relating to the Irish health services, and these reflect the strategic principles outlined above. These themes are also supported in recent legislative changes pertaining to the planning, funding and delivery of health services.

Theme 1
The need to refocus health services (prevention, treatment and care services) on effectiveness and appropriateness
There is a shift in thinking from the provision of treatment to prevention. This is reflected in an emphasis on improving the health status and the quality of life of individuals and the population as a whole and on the need to measure effectiveness of health services in improving health outcomes. There is increasing interest in the prevention and early detection of illness, and on empowering individuals to take ownership of their own well being and to positively influence health behaviour.

In providing preventative services, screening, treatment and care, there is also an increasing awareness of the need to assess and evaluate what forms of treatment are most effective and appropriate in response to different needs. The challenge is then to make these findings available to decision makers and to ensure that service provision is focused on those identified.

In addition, there is an interest in how services and expertise can be used most effectively. Examples include the appropriate use of services such as accident and emergency and outpatient services, where it might be more appropriate for GPs to be paid a fee to carry out minor surgery; the use of day-patient services in place of in-patient care for less complex procedures; and the appropriate use of support personnel to free up expertise that could be better used – for example, using nurses rather than doctors to do routine child health examinations.

Responsive and appropriate care delivery is one of the four goals of the 2001 *Health Strategy*. The approach outlined is aimed at gearing the health system to respond appropriately, adequately and in a timely way to the needs of individuals and families, ensuring that all parts of the system are being used effectively and efficiently. This includes developing integrated approaches to care planning for individuals and efforts to ensure that care is delivered in the most appropriate setting. The development of evidence-based approaches to the delivery of care is also promoted in the strategy.

Theme 2

The need to update management and organisation structures

Separating policy from operational management. The Commission on Health Funding (1989) suggested that current structures confused political and executive functions. *Shaping a Healthier Future* recommended that the department should devolve several of its functions to health boards to enable it to refocus efforts on policy, while devolving decision making to regional level. The Health (Amendment) Act (1996) and the Eastern Regional Health Authority Act (1998) set out the provisions for such separation and clarified the responsibility of the health boards /ERHA in the new structures.

Enhancing and strengthening accountability at all levels of the system. This was reflected particularly in the accountability legislation introduced in 1996, which sought to clarify the respective roles of the department, the health boards (both board members and managers) and other agencies (see the earlier outline of this legislation).

Enhancing the effectiveness of decision making. The devolution of decision making to regional/local level is aimed at achieving the 'proper balance between local and national decision making' (Report of Commission on Health Funding, 1989). The thinking is that the closer decisions are made to those who use them, the more relevant they will be and the more responsive services will be to population and individual needs.

The current deficit in information and evaluation in health service management is noted in many policy documents. The 1989 Report of the Commission on Health Funding suggests that allocation decisions are made without sufficient knowledge of the consequences and are based on intuitive rather than objective criteria. Butler (2000) argues that along with deficits in information and evaluation, there are deficits in relation to the appropriate use of data in decision making.

More recently there is an increasing awareness of the need to take a longer-term and strategic view in planning health services and this is reflected in one of the Department of Health and Children's objectives: 'to plan the strategic development of services in consultation and partnership between the Department of Health and Children, health boards, the voluntary sector and other relevant government departments or interests' (see

Department of Health and Children, 1998, p. 8). The new health strategy aims to improve the performance of the health system by developing an evidence-based, strategic approach to decisionmaking at all levels.

Better integration of services. New structures also seek to improve the integration of care. The provision of holistic, patient-centred care, based on close teamwork between health professionals and direct access to services, is a key theme in the new strategy. Integration is promoted both across sectors, for example between primary and hospital services, and within sectors. The development of the primary care sector will include the development of primary care teams and networks which are designed to give primary care providers greater capacity to meet the range of needs for each individual. In the acute sector, the 2001 strategy also seeks to achieve more integrated care

> An integrated approach to care planning for individuals will become a consistent feature of the system. Lack of integration of care between and even within some services is identified as a problem in the existing services. For example, older people may be cared for in acute wards due to the unavailability of more appropriate community supports. Individual patients or clients may have to access the system several times to have all their needs addressed. This may apply within the hospital system where individuals have needs involving a number of specialties. If the system is to be responsive to the needs of individuals, it is important that a holistic approach is taken to planning and delivering care. This will include: greater communication and liaison between individual clinicians within services and across services; development of care management approaches involving packages of care for groups with multiple needs; and the appointment of key workers in the context of care planning, in particular, for dependent older people such as those on the margins of home and residential care; and for children with disabilities.

(Department of Health and Children, 2001a, p.81)

Theme 3
The need to improve the focus on the consumer
The importance of a customer-focused approach was stressed in the 1994 *Health Strategy* and in subsequent departmental strategy

statements. People-centredness is also a key theme in the new strategy. Key dimensions of a consumer/customer-focused approach include: the development of a customer service ethos in the delivery of health services; highlighting the rights of patients and the need for quality services that are responsive to needs; carrying out patient satisfaction surveys; comprehensiveness, equity and cost-effectiveness in service provision; representation of the interests of patients and clients within the health care structures.

STRUCTURE OF THE BOOK

This examination of Irish healthcare reforms is not intended to be exhaustive but to highlight the range of key issues currently facing health service planners, policy makers and managers in the provision and funding of health services in Ireland: issues where the experience of other countries is of great interest. This chapter has sought to set the scene for the more detailed exploration of several of these issues in subsequent chapters. The purpose of this book is not to rewrite or update what is to be found in the burgeoning literature on comparative health care, but to explore Irish issues from a comparative perspective. As such, it should be seen as complementary to other texts and journal articles. This book attempts to demonstrate, by way of practical example, the benefits of comparative analysis and to provide a useful source of reference material for health policy students in Ireland who might wish to conduct a comparative review of any health management issue.

Chapter 2 looks at the benefits of comparative study in general, while Chapter 3 gives a brief and necessarily selective guide to a vast comparative literature. The subsequent chapters look at specific issues in Ireland against the background of international trends: health gain, service planning, performance measurement, quality management, the public-private mix and the voluntary sector.

A concluding chapter will then briefly reflect on some lessons to be learnt from this comparative review.

Chapter 2
The Benefits of Comparative Healthcare Study

Comparative health care, as a subject, has found its way into many course curricula and has recently featured in Internet programmes (Rathwell et al, 1999): a testament to the increasing recognition of its importance. However, the case for comparative study in health care policy and management needs to be clearly articulated in Ireland. Comparison with Britain is part of our tradition, but the case for wider comparison is less well appreciated. Anyone seeking to make that case must address some core questions. How do we compare different systems? What do we compare? What can we in Ireland learn from other health care systems? What can people in other systems learn from us?

This chapter seeks to address these questions and then to examine some more general comparative health lessons which arise from reflection on these questions. It begins with a brief definition of comparative health care and a discussion of possible frameworks for comparison. The next chapter looks at some current literature and sources on comparative healthcare.

As Higgins (1981) notes, comparative policy is not a separate field of study. It is a method of public policy study, which uses comparison in a systematic way to highlight influences on, features and consequences of policy. Comparison in health care or elsewhere springs from the basic reality that it would be difficult to analyse any policy or institutional arrangement without considering existing or possible alternatives.

The advantages of comparative study have been well summarised by Jones (1985) among others. She refers to benefits such as better understanding, a broadening of ideas and the identification of lessons from abroad; and to the development of a greater breadth and variety of case material (p. 4). One significant advantage of comparative study is that it helps to identify important issues for consideration by policy makers. These include (to list a few) funding and eligibility; legal and ethical issues; performance measurement; health service outcomes and the achievement of health gain; service planning in healthcare; quality in healthcare; the doctor-patient relationship; the relationship between the medical and nursing professions and the state; the implications of demographic trends; the public-private mix; statutory-voluntary relationships; health and disease trends; and the reform process in general.

No comparative study should become submerged in the details of the systems it considers but must, at the risk of over-simplification, attempt to arrive at a more general understanding of the features and operation of the systems concerned. Comparative studies lead ultimately to some sort of typology or classification of systems – to the identification of possible frameworks within which different systems may be compared. A framework of this type may be seen as a tool for comparing different healthcare systems. It helps one to think about the health services in one's own country and elsewhere. A significant benefit of comparative study is therefore that it may produce a useful framework for thinking about the health services. Some of these frameworks are discussed in Chapter 3.

COMPARATIVE EXAMINATION OF HEALTH CARE OBJECTIVES

One approach to comparative health study is to compare health care objectives or principles. Thus, on the basis of core principles (care of the needy or vulnerable; respect for life; competence of care; efficiency; ease of access) one might compare how far concrete health services reflect the application of such principles. In the Irish context, one might look at how well Irish health services reflect the core principles of equity, quality and accountability set out in the 1994 *Health Strategy*.

Alternatively – and this is undoubtedly a less daunting task – one might compare existing stated objectives, mission statements and philosophical statements in different countries. This somewhat less challenging task will be attempted below.

Official Irish statements of health services philosophy are comparatively rare. One such statement may be found in the quasi-official report of the Commission on Health Funding (1989). This report identified two fundamental precepts or principles in health services – that necessary health services should be available to all persons on the basis of their need and not of their ability to pay: and that the costs of such services should be shared on the principle of proportionately greater contributions from those of greater means (par. 6.18). Similar principles were set out in the influential white paper on the health services in 1966 (Department of Health, 1966). The practical application of these principles in Ireland today is that all persons are now entitled to free hospital services here, though only 30 per cent are entitled to free GMS services.

In 1994, the *Health Strategy* emphasised the guiding principles of equity, quality and accountability and the objective of achieving health gain and social gain. The main theme of the strategy was

> ... the reorientation of the system towards improving the effectiveness of the health and personal social services by reshaping the way that services are planned and delivered (p. 8).

How is health services philosophy expressed elsewhere? In their study of healthcare reform in Europe, Saltman and Figueras (1997) highlight major 'societal norms' or values in Europe relating to healthcare. These are social solidarity, the role of the state and accountability. In their view, the value of social solidarity continues to be more influential in Europe than does market-based thinking. They refer to the strong state role in some European countries, which, they argue, has been legitimised by free democratic elections.

Saltman and Figueras also assert that there is potential tension between different objectives. In most democratic societies, they argue, three major values are in tension with each other: equity, individual autonomy and efficiency. They highlight conflicting principles such as social solidarity, equity and health status, on the one hand, and cost containment on the other.

Are different health care objectives compatible with each other? Are cost containment and competition compatible with access and equity? Can the Irish *Health Strategy* principles of equity, quality and accountability be reconciled? An important comparative issue in examining objectives is this question of conflict between objectives.

Ham (1997) argues (p. 15) that policies designed to increase efficiency, choice and responsiveness may make it difficult to achieve objectives such as access and equity. In his view, the challenge for policy makers in this situation is to make trade-offs between different objectives.

The OECD (1996) argues however that it is important not to exaggerate conflict between objectives

> In many cases, improved efficiency will be consistent with equity, since access is improved when efficiency increases. Many technological improvements in medicine are of this type, though not all. It is, in fact, unethical to be inefficient, since this deprives some individuals of healthcare that otherwise could have been delivered (p. 32).

The reform process

Saltman and Figueras (1997) take the debate on objectives further by examining the reform process. Their focus is not so much on objectives per se but rather on the reform process in general. Much recent writing on comparative healthcare – for example, the works of Raffel (1997) or the Healthcare Systems in Transition series of the WHO – has focused on this theme of reform. A significant benefit of recent comparative study is that it promotes a better understanding of the reform process.

Saltman and Figueras (1997) provide a detailed definition of reform:

> Reform is defined as a process that involves sustained and profound institutional and structural change, led by government and seeking to attain a series of explicit policy objectives (p. 3).

They also set out a series of key elements of healthcare reform, stressing that reform is about the implementation, and not merely the redefinition of objectives. They point to key conditions for the successful implementation of reforms. These include timing, financial sustainability, political will and leadership, strategic alliances, public support, managing the process and technical infrastructure and capacity (p. 259). Their analysis of reform requirements is based on an analysis of the reform experience in different European countries, including Ireland.

IRELAND'S LEARNING FROM OTHER HEALTH SYSTEMS

Irish interest in comparative health care has focused on practical lessons to be learnt rather than on an examination of health care models in a wider sense. A partial exception to this general approach might be the report of the Commission on Health Funding (1989), which considered, albeit briefly, whether social insurance-based funding on the continental European model might constitute an alternative in Ireland to funding through general taxation.

It would be impossible in a short space to summarise Irish learning in health services over the last few decades. In the clinical area, many Irish health service professionals undertake some of their training abroad. Irish managers and policy makers are members of many EU health services committees. The focus here is on a few practical examples from the management and policy spheres.

American, and more specifically British, perspectives on and approaches to management have been very influential in Ireland. Indeed the management structures of the new health boards in 1971 were based on the recommendations of London-based international management consultants, McKinseys. The current management development strategy for the Irish health services was written by two British experts on management, Dixon and Baker (1996).

The health gain approach espoused by the 1994 *Health Strategy* owes much to WHO thinking (on 'adding years to life' and 'life to years') (WHO, 1995) and to specific initiatives such as health gain developments and reports in Wales, for example the publications of the Welsh Health Planning Forum (1989).

In the area of private health insurance, the Australian model has proved of interest. Irish health insurance experts studied the Australian experience; it is at least arguable that the ongoing Irish commitment to community rating was influenced by the difficulties experienced in Australia health insurance when community rating was undermined because (among other reasons) of the entry of commercial insurers operating risk-rating policies into the marketplace (see Schneider, 1999).

Funding for acute hospitals based on casemix and particularly on the Diagnosis Related Groups mechanism, developed in the US in the 1980s, was studied with interest in Ireland and came to the Irish acute hospital services in 1993 (Fitzgerald and Lynch, 1998).

The application of economic ideas and frameworks and language to the Irish health services has been developing since the 1970s. Of significance here, for example, was the work of Tussing (1985), an American economist, who applied economic notions of supplier-induced demand to the Irish health services, and possibly contributed to the change in the method of funding of GPs in 1989.

What lessons might Ireland learn in the years ahead from other systems? One area of interest is to look at emerging organisational structures in other countries. Some of the new quality and accreditation structures are examined in Chapter 8.

In the 1990s, in some publicly funded – more specifically, tax-funded – health care systems, there was an attempt, under the influence of market concepts (often rooted in US experience), to move from what were perceived as unresponsive, top-heavy structures towards more responsive, consumer-oriented health care delivery.

In Britain, the change followed the white paper *Working for Patients* in 1989. Where previously the same body (for example, a district health authority) both funded and directly delivered services – for example, in one of its own acute hospitals – now a separation was established between the purchaser, the health authority and the provider, the hospital. The latter was re-established as a trust and given greater autonomy. New purchasing organisations – GP fund-holders – were also established in general practice.

These changes aroused interest in Ireland. While the British reforms after 1989 were viewed with some reserve here, NHS initiatives in relation to purchaser-provider splits also aroused interest and arguably had some influence on the commissioner-provider split which was introduced in 2000 to the new Eastern Regional Health Authority (between the ERHA and provider agencies in the region).

Such changes were not confined to Britain. Harrison and Calltorp (2000) state that Sweden was an important pioneer of market-oriented reforms in publicly-funded health care systems. In Sweden, where decentralised health care provision was based around the counties, experiments in purchaser-provider separation developed from the early 1990s.

In New Zealand, another tax-funded, integrated system, developments in purchaser-provider separation followed the 1993 Health and Disability Services Act. Ritchie (1998) notes that that Act provided the legislative basis in New Zealand for substantive organisational changes including the separation of the purchaser and provider roles, integration of primary and secondary care and the definition of core services.

The changes of the 1990s however were subject to significant review later in the decade. In Britain, a change in government in 1997 brought with it changes in the structures established following the 1989 white paper. Thus, changes occurred in the nature of health care purchasers. Primary care groups (PCGs) were established to replace the GP fund-holders. The PCGs were intended to include all GPs and community nurses in an area and not just a proportion of the GPs as before. Similarly, where the virtues of competition had been particularly stressed prior to 1997, now the emphasis was on integration and cooperation. Nevertheless, the principle of purchaser-provider separation was seen as valuable and was retained.

In Sweden, by the mid-1990s, according to Harrison and Calltorp (2000)

> ... the county councils, which fund and manage most health care, had substantially scaled back most reforms based on provider competition while continuing to constrain health budgets. As policy makers faced new issues, they turned increasingly to longer-term and more cooperative contracts to define relations between hospitals and the county councils (p. 219).

Market concepts and mechanisms remain influential in health care but perhaps less so than a decade ago. The current comparative health care literature includes reflections on alternative/complementary concepts and approaches. Thus Saltman and Ferroussier-Davis (2000), in an article for a WHO publication, advocate the concept of 'stewardship' as an appropriate concept for governments 'responsible for the welfare of populations and concerned about the trust and legitimacy with which its activities are viewed by the general public' (p. 735). They argue that:

> Stewardship involves an emphasis on good outcomes in the European style rather than a concentration predominantly on transparent processes in the style of the USA (p. 736).

Structural reforms in social insurance funded systems took a somewhat different form from those in tax-funded systems. For one thing, a certain distinction already existed in the social insurance systems between funding and provision of services. In Germany, for example, there already existed a distinction between the funder of services (the sickness funds) and the providers (the hospitals and the professional associations). It is debatable however whether sickness funds, in Germany or elsewhere, were traditionally active purchasers of care in the manner envisaged in some of the reforms described above.

In Ireland, partly because of a traditional focus on British and American experiences, and partly because of the different funding systems in continental Europe, we have traditionally paid less attention to continental European health systems; but there is undoubtedly a case for studying their experience more carefully in the future.

The 1993 Health Care Structure Act was an important policy change in Germany. It established competition between sickness funds. Previously, German citizens enjoyed a wide choice of provider but not a choice of sickness fund. Since the 1993 Act, this choice of funds and competition between funds has led to a merger between some funds as they seek to equip themselves for competition.

An important theme of health care reform in Germany has been contribution stability. With health care funding coming from the workplace (from both employer and employee), an objective of policy has been to limit the rate of growth of such contributions so that German industry remains competitive at an international level (Schwartz and Busse, 1997).

Similar preoccupations apply to the French social insurance system, which experienced serious funding deficits in the mid-1990s. In the French reforms of the 1990s, the contribution of taxation was increased so that it now plays a bigger role in the funding of the health care system than it did previously.

In the French social insurance system, there was traditionally a good deal of delegation by government to the social partners (employers and trade unions) who ran the sickness funds. However, under funding pressures in the mid-1990s, new structures and approaches developed which amounted to tighter central control of healthcare funding and delivery. More specifically, greater parliamentary control of the healthcare system was reflected in the establishment of global budgets/global expenditure ceilings and a requirement for annual parliamentary approval of healthcare objectives and priorities.

Under the Juppé reforms of the mid-1990s, new hospital agencies were also established – the ARH or regional hospital agencies. These agencies are required to regulate all hospitals, both public and private, in their region and to develop multi-annual contracts with such hospitals. In France as elsewhere, service integration was an important objective of health care reform.

New experimental networks were also established in France under the Juppé reforms. These networks – known as *filières or réseaux* – are experiments in the establishment of gatekeeper GP provision, or in the provision of coordinated care for people with chronic or resource-intensive conditions such as AIDS, where such service coordination is crucial.

These care networks are in effect experiments in care provision which are funded by the social security system. The policy objective is to learn appropriate lessons from such experiments. The experiments seek to offer incentives to all sides – the social insurance funder, the providers and the patients – so that all have a vested interest in their success.

Ireland has traditionally had a centralised tradition of government. Some of the reforms of recent years have sought to devolve authority from the centre to the regions. The existing regional structures in health care have been in existence for thirty years and have been under review in the new strategy preparation process. For all these reasons, decentralisation is an important current theme in Irish health services.

Decentralisation is also an important theme of structural reform in other countries. Saltman and Figueras (1997) argue that the reason for international interest in decentralisation is 'widespread disillusion with large, centralised and bureaucratic institutions' (p. 43). They identify (pp. 44-45) four types of decentralisation: *deconcentration* (transfer of decision making to a lower administrative level); *devolution* (such transfer to a lower political level); *delegation* (the allocation of defined tasks to actors at a lower organisational level), and *privatisation* (the transfer of authority and functions from the public to the private sector – though they see this as very different from the other forms of decentralisation).

Decentralisation is not necessarily a simple phenomenon. For instance, centralisation and decentralisation may occur simultaneously in a given country. Thus in France, parliament assumed somewhat greater control in the 1990s over the social security system in which there had traditionally been very significant delegation to the social partners involved in running the sickness funds. On the other hand, the 1990s also witnessed the establishment of significant new regional structures in France such as the regional hospital agencies.

Canada is another example of a country which experienced significant decentralisation in the 1990s. Canadian decentralisation was from the provinces to regions within the provinces. In developing such decentralisation, Lomas (1997) argues, provincial governments had the objectives of developing community empowerment to gain new allies for health restructuring, service integration and conflict containment as spending was cut.

With decentralisation, it was hoped (among other objectives) that provincial governments would face less controversy as difficult spending cutbacks were introduced. There has been much Canadian debate about the motivation for decentralisation (how influential, for example, was the desire to contain costs?) and about its impact.

As in France, centralisation and decentralisation occurred at the same time in Canada. As Naylor (1999) puts it, 'even as provincial ministries devolve some administrative authority and budgetary elements to regions, the emergence of regional authorities centralises administrative control at the expense of individual institutions and agencies within a region' (p. 14).

Naylor notes that there is no 'model' decentralised structure in Canada: there is, he argues, interprovincial variation in how regional boards are appointed or elected, in the population size within regions and in the extent to which regions have integrated health services.

In their report for the WHO, Saltman and Figueras (1997) review the advantages and disadvantages of decentralisation in the European countries they survey and argue that that 'decentralising responsibilities while maintaining a degree of central influence appears to be the optimum form of decentralisation for many countries' (p. 55). They note that decentralisation is often favoured as a means of improving the coordination of services and activities at local level and add: 'It also reflects the recognition that health is more than health care and that other agencies outside the health care system must be involved in reshaping the policy agenda' (p. 55).

Their overall verdict is that the jury is out on the impact of decentralisation:

The outcome of decentralisation has not often been evaluated in the light of health gain, equity, efficiency, quality of care and consumer choice. Decision makers have typically taken it for granted that decentralisation automatically brings about positive changes, and assumed that there is no need for evaluation. Furthermore, the expected outcomes are often not well-defined in advance. It would be a major step forward if policy makers could define explicitly what kinds of improvement were expected from decentralisation policies (pp. 56 and 58).

Ireland's interest in HR developments in other countries

There is a link between the structural developments outlined in the previous section and human resource (HR) issues. Changes in structures may lead to demands for new types of personnel or new types of competence. Thus Ritchie (1998) argues that the separation of purchaser and provider roles reinforced the need for a new style of management giving greater emphasis to information, service provision, organisation structure and development and broader resource management issues (p. 184). Ritchie refers to a related shift in countries like New Zealand, Australia and Britain, from a traditional 'passive' health management style (using 'transactional' management skills to balance historically-based expenditure budgets) to more 'active' goal-oriented, transformational leadership styles with a stronger 'private sector' or market orientation.

Fleming (2000) also links structural and HR issues and developments. Public sector organisations, she writes, are increasingly recognising that 'cultural change, as a means of developing responsible and adaptable structures, can only be achieved through innovative policies for the management of *human* as well as financial resources' (p. 7). She notes that the concept of Human Resource Management (HRM), as a new strategic approach to the management of people, evolved in the early 1980s. Citing Storey (1989), Fleming points to four features of HRM which distinguish it from traditional personnel management. It is explicitly linked with corporate strategy. It seeks to obtain the commitment of employees rather than their compliance. Such commitment is obtained through an integrated approach to human resource policies (covering, for example, reward, appraisal, selection and training). Unlike personnel management, which is primarily the domain of specialists, HRM is owned by line managers as a means of fostering integration (p. 8).

Fleming (2000) identifies the key lessons from international experience of HRM public sector reform as being: the decentralisation of HRM (from central to line departments) and the development of an integrated approach to HRM at line department level; the devolution of HRM (from personnel sections to line managers) and the professionalisation of the HR function. International experience, she states, suggests that the key challenge lies in granting departments adequate freedom to manage financial and human resources, facilitating the development of best practice HRM, while at the same time retaining appropriate control of the essentials at the centre (p. 52).

Humphreys and Worth-Butler (1999), based on their review of the international literature, argue that in HRM terms the key needs are for: strategic planning to meet current and future needs of the service; stronger management; devolution of responsibility and accountability for recruitment and personnel management; partnership and collaborative working; responsive/flexible systems; the introduction/development of performance management; and the promotion of new ways of working.

The comparative health care literature suggests that major HR issues in health care in OECD countries include, ageing labour forces and ageing populations, shortages of key professionals, difficulties in their recruitment and retention and pressures to contain personnel costs.

The Canadian Institute for Health Information (2000) highlighted problems such as: ageing health care professionals; fewer young people entering the professions; work stress; and absenteeism.

UK problems include major nursing shortages, the lack of coordination of strategies between different authorities – for example, in relation to GP recruitment (see Young and Leese 1999) – and problems in recruiting senior managers.

The provisions of the NHS Plan 2000 have important HR provisions. As well as promising an increase of UK funding to the EU average and establishing specific waiting times for key services, the plan provides for an increase in the numbers of doctors and nurses and for changes to the contracts of key professionals such as hospital consultants.

McGauran (2001) states that under the current NHS Human Resources Strategy, health authorities will be required to report their progress on childcare strategies, local recruitment drives, career breaks, attempts to tackle the long-hours culture and progress on quality and diversity.

Overseas recruitment of key professionals is also assuming increased importance in Britain and elsewhere.

In relation to HR capacity-building in the health services, recurring themes in the literature – for example, McGauran (2001), Gray and Phillips (1995) – include: family-friendly policies and flexibility of conditions; local autonomy; incentives for self-development; recognition of good performance; training for new recruits; career counseling; targeted retention policies (for example, retention of women); information systems (including such data as the results of exit interviews); leadership preparation and training; and skill mix.

Some of these themes have been suggested on the basis of a comparison (see for example, Gray and Phillips, 1995) between health service employers and successful employers in other areas. A key underlying theme is the importance of focus on quality and of seeing HR initiatives in the context of such a focus.

LEARNING FROM THE IRISH EXPERIENCE

The last section has looked at possible Irish learning from developments elsewhere. Which aspects of the Irish health services experience have proved of most interest elsewhere? International interest in Ireland in the 1990s has focused on the 'Celtic Tiger', the Irish 'economic miracle', but has been less evident in relation to the Irish health services.

Nevertheless, a study by the OECD (1997) of the Irish health system presented Ireland as an example of a country which provided a good standard of healthcare on the basis of a judicious mixture of public and private health services. The OECD highlighted the sharp cutbacks in spending in the 1980s and the role of private health insurance in the Irish system.

The Irish approach to private health insurance – and more specifically, the experience of the VHI, a body established by the state – has aroused interest in central Europe, where societies are moving from a socialist system of healthcare towards more market-based systems. For countries emerging from state-controlled domination of the medical profession, the Irish tradition of a self-regulating medical profession and the role of the Medical Council, or of An Bord Altranais in relation to nursing, may also prove of interest (see Hensey 1988 pp. 155ff).

In the future, international interest in the Irish health services is likely to focus on issues which are universally of concern: for example, cost containment, the involvement of the professions in management, accountability and the state and the market.

However, it is possible to point to a number of areas where Ireland's experience may be of particular interest. One such area is the involvement of voluntary agencies in the Irish health services: both the larger public voluntary hospitals and mental handicap agencies and smaller voluntary bodies − for example, local care of the elderly associations. With the growth of international interest in the non-profit sector, as reported by Salamon and Anheier (1997) of the Johns Hopkins project it is likely that Ireland's experience in this area will also prove of interest. Donoghue, Salamon and Anheier (1999) have begun to report on some work applying the Johns Hopkins categories to Ireland (see Chapter 9).

Interest in statutory-voluntary links in Ireland may focus on Irish developments such as the negotiation of the agreement *Enhancing the Partnership* (Department of Health and Children, 1997), between the state and the large mental handicap agencies.

The public-private mix in Ireland is also likely to prove of ongoing interest in other countries. The OECD (1997) thus summarised some unusual features of the Irish system

> Until 1996, the health insurance-based sector has operated as part of the broader state health system. Indeed, since its establishment, the VHI is therefore unique and has been operated in a way that tries to ensure that a significant number of people stay in the private system, so minimising the cost of hospital care to public finances (p. 125).

Interest in the future is likely to focus on how the Irish private health insurance system has responded to competition and to the emergence of a second major insurer (BUPA). Light (1998) has already given a US perspective on recent policy debate on this area in Ireland.

Other areas of considerable interest will doubtless include the Irish nursing reforms, for example the move to a nursing degree for all student nurses by 2002; the impact of Irish accountability legislation and of particular accountability mechanisms such as service planning; and the success or otherwise of clinicians in management initiatives.

There may be international interest in the philosophical debate in Ireland about health care objectives, fundamental right-to-life issues, the values of healthcare professionals or the ethics of resource allocation in the health services. Bioethical issues – ethical issues relating to the status of human life at its beginning and end – are requiring more and more urgent attention and reflection throughout Europe.

LESSONS FROM COMPARISON

The aims of this chapter have been to suggest that there is much to be learnt from comparative study in health care; that Irish health services personnel have learned a lot from the study of health services developments elsewhere; and that there has also been significant international interest in the Irish experience.

Comparative study in health care raises broad issues. How does one compare health care systems? Which methods of classification are appropriate? Does one focus for example on the role of the state? How does one analyse that role? This chapter has looked at these questions without exploring their more theoretical aspects.

The focus here has been more on practical questions. Which services do we compare? Which issues do we consider? What is the possible learning from such comparison?

This chapter listed at the outset some issues which comparative study helps to identify. These issues can be re-phrased in the form of critical questions to be faced by Irish policy makers (but of relevance elsewhere as well). How can health services be re-oriented to achieve optimum health gain? What possible frameworks exist for service planning and performance measurement in the health services? How do current approaches help to achieve quality in the health services? How can the patient be involved more effectively in decision making in the health services? What are the appropriate roles of the public and private sectors and of statutory and voluntary sectors?

These and other questions will be looked at in more detail throughout this text.

As this chapter has argued, the examination of all these questions, and policy developments in relation to them, are enriched and helped by comparative study in health care. The next chapter provides a brief guide to some relevant literature.

Chapter 3
A Selective Guide to
the Literature

The literature on comparative healthcare is vast and growing and today includes an enormous range of websites on the Internet. No one could claim familiarity with more than a fraction of this material. This chapter seeks simply to provide a selective guide, from an Irish perspective, to some of this literature and to some of the themes which it covers.

The comparative literature presents theoretical and practical classifications of health care systems. This chapter will look briefly at each of these areas in turn.

THEORETICAL FRAMEWORKS

Much writing about comparative healthcare attempts to provide a typology or classification of systems – in other words, to identify possible frameworks within which different systems can be compared. Some of this vast literature attempts to provide a framework for theorising about the welfare state in general; some of it focuses specifically on health systems.

A detailed discussion of theoretical models of comparative health care is outside the scope of this chapter, indeed of this book. Rather, we will refer to a number of models, some of which focus on the role of the state. Thus an influential recent theorist, Esping-Andersen (1990) distinguishes between conservative, socialist and liberal regimes. Other theorists such as Roemer (1977) and Field (1989) make similar distinctions. Field distinguishes between emergent, pluralistic, insurance/social security, national health service and socialised systems.

International classifications of the welfare state do not necessarily adopt a neutral position in relation to the different categories of welfare regime which they identify. Traditionally, many theorists advocated a strong state role and made the case, whether explicitly or not, for the superiority of welfare regimes in social democratic states. For example, Cochrane and Clarke (1993) argue that conservative welfare regimes tend to dominate in those countries in which Catholic parties are strong, parties of the left weak and where there has been a strong history of 'absolutism and authoritarianism' (p8). They adopt a more positive approach towards social-democratic regimes which, they maintain, are characterised by principles of 'universalism and equality': 'This regime tends to encourage equality across classes, based on high standards, rather than the minima endorsed elsewhere' (p.9).

However, any favourable consensus in the literature in relation to a specific role for the state has been shaken by the sweeping social changes of recent decades. Wilding (1992) and Johnson (1987) have documented some of these changes in the British context.

Writers such as Ó Cinnéide (1993), O'Connell and Rottman (1992) and Cousins (1997) examine different typologies of welfare state systems and how Ireland fits into them – for example, Esping-Andersen's three-fold typology of conservative, liberal and social democratic regimes. Cochrane and Clarke (1993) examine whether the Republic of Ireland embodies or did embody 'the characteristics of a Catholic corporatist welfare regime' – described as a variant of Esping-Andersen's conservative corporatist welfare regime (p. 205). Fanning (1999) and O'Donnell (1999) provide a useful guide to some of the literature on comparative healthcare typologies, even if O'Donnell stresses the difficulty of 'fitting Ireland in' to any particular framework.

Ó Cinnéide (1993) identifies a number of possible frameworks for comparative theorising about the welfare state in an EU context: theories related to classification of existing welfare states; theories relating to how welfare states have developed; theories relating to ideologies which inform welfare state policies and theories of European Community policy making. He refers for example to the models outlined by Esping-Andersen (1990), Room (1979) and George and Wilding (1976). He raises the question: 'To what extent is the Irish welfare state distinctive and different?' and responds: 'The fact that Ireland is peripheral, recently industrialising and Catholic is assumed to have determined the kind of welfare state that exists in Ireland' (p.99).

However, Ó Cinnéide argues that there are deficiencies in this argument, including the fact that the Irish welfare state has more in common with its neighbour, Britain, than with other 'peripheral' countries of Europe. Ó Cinnéide finds more convincing the arguments of O'Connell and Rottman (1992). They discuss different explanatory models for the development of welfare states – for example, 'the logic of industrialism', 'social democratic influence' and the 'state-centred approach'. They view this third model as most relevant to Ireland. In other words, they point to the key role played by the state itself (as distinct from other possible actors such as the trade unions, the Church or the process of industrialisation) in the development of welfare services in Ireland.

Theoretical frameworks are useful in so far as they explain developments in social security and more specifically in health systems. Our aim here is not to offer a judgement on the different theoretical models but simply to give some sense of their range and variety.

PRACTICAL FRAMEWORKS

As well as theoretical classification of welfare states, comparative literature also provides more practical, policy-oriented frameworks. For example, Saltman and Figueras (1997) offer a classification of healthcare systems which is based on politics and economics. They divide the health systems of Europe into three categories: the countries of Western Europe, the former Soviet-bloc countries of Central and Eastern Europe (CEE) (for example, Poland) and the newly independent states of the former USSR (CIS).

While they do not reflect in depth on the justification for this classification, the authors are implicitly stressing the importance of politics, economic development and health trends respectively – that is, the three areas in which there are major differences between these three sets of countries. By politics, they refer not simply to the role of the state but also to democratic traditions, which are stronger in Western Europe than in the other regions they consider.

The OECD (1995 and 1996) is an important source for practical comparison of healthcare systems based, for example, on their levels of healthcare spending. Its international statistics, for example, present Ireland's total and public spending as a percentage of GDP in the context of international data on such spending.

Many classifications of healthcare systems focus on the type of funding system chosen – a decision which ultimately rests with the state. In a practical administrative classification of healthcare systems, Ham (1997, p.4) distinguishes between:

• public finance based on general taxation (for example, Britain, New Zealand, the Nordic Countries)
• public finance based on compulsory social insurance (for example, Germany, the Netherlands, France and Belgium) and
• private finance based on voluntary insurance (for example, the United States).

Ireland could be assigned to the first of these groups, as public funding in Ireland is largely tax-based. On the other hand, Ireland differs in that private insurance plays a very important role in its healthcare system and universal health services coverage does not apply in Ireland. For example, GP services are provided free to just 30 per cent of the population. In relation to the US, one should also mention publicly-funded programmes such as Medicare and Medicaid.

The OECD (1992) identifies a number of possible sub-systems of financing and delivery of health care (p.19) based on interactions between five principal 'sets of actors' in health care systems. The details of the sub-systems are beyond the scope of this chapter but it is useful to refer to the key actors identified by the OECD: the consumers/patients; the first-level providers (such as GPs); the second-level providers (such as most hospital services); the insurers or third-party payers; and the government in its capacity as regulator of the system.

In the OECD framework, comparison was then carried out on the basis of a study of the interactions between different actors. A similar approach was taken by Paton (2000). In an analysis of EU countries, Paton describes three types of system.

The 'Bismarck' systems of continental Europe (for example, Germany and Belgium) have various 'quasi-public' payers (sickness funds) to which people subscribe on the basis of criteria such as occupation; and public money is used to pay for most if not all care or services. The name comes from the German Chancellor who pioneered social insurance.

The 'Beveridge' system (named after the British social reformer of the 1940s) which combines public provision with 'single payer' financing from general revenues (examples: United Kingdom and Sweden).

Finally, Paton identifies a 'mixed' group – for example, Ireland and France.

In Paton's view countries such as Ireland and France do not quite fit into the other two categories. In Ireland, he argues, a major part (though not all) of the system is essentially of the Beveridge type, while France is a social insurance system on the Bismarck model, but is evolving in a somewhat different direction to Bismarck countries such as Germany which have given a greater policy priority to competition (notably, between sickness funds)

COMMENT ON FRAMEWORKS

No method of classification of health care systems (whether theoretical or practical) will be entirely satisfactory or above criticism. The classifications just discussed do not, for example, devote much attention to differences (or similarities) in policy on fundamental ethical issues; or to the nature of the doctor-patient relationship (see May, 1983) in different systems; nor do they give much consideration to the role of non-profit or voluntary organisations.

Nevertheless, what is important in any method of classification is its fruitfulness as a tool for empirical investigation or for opening important lines of enquiry. For example, the classification of Saltman and Figueras has proved a fruitful way of examining the reform process in recent years in different European countries and is based on detailed policy assessments from across the three 'regions' of Europe which they identify.

SOME USEFUL SOURCES IN THE LITERATURE

In relation to funding and expenditure, the OECD is the main source of information for health spending trends in OECD countries. OECD texts include, for example: *Health Systems. Facts and Trends* (1992); *The Reform of Healthcare Systems,* (1994); *New Directions in Health Care Policy,* (1995); and *Health Care Reform. The Will to Change* (1996).

The OECD database, *Health Data*, is also a very important source of information. Calculations on a wide variety of expenditure categories can be carried out on this database.

Health spending in Europe is covered in recent WHO publications , for example, the study by Saltman and Figueras (1997), *European Healthcare Reform* and the *World Health Report* of the WHO (2000). Saltman and Figueras note that health spending increased in Western Europe in the 1960s and 1970s , was stable in the 1980s but that in the 1990s there was a small upturn in spending.

In examining cost containment measures, they distinguish between supply-oriented and demand-oriented measures. They give as examples of supply-oriented measures: spending caps, reduction in the number of hospital beds or in numbers of doctors and medical students; substitution policies, controls over expensive medical equipment, control of use of resources authorised by physicians, for example medical references in France, which specify the use of drug prescriptions related to a specific health condition.

They provide the following examples of demand oriented measures: cost sharing; opting out in compulsory health insurance systems; no-claims bonuses; reductions in services; and rationing (for example, through waiting times)

The World Bank has also provided information on health spending in developing countries and has compared such spending with spending in richer countries. A useful World Bank source is its website: http://www.worldbank.org/healthreform

The WHO also has statistical information on each country in its annual World Health Report. This is also available on the Internet: www.who.int. The WHO and the European Observatory on Health Care Systems publish the health care systems in transition (HITS) series. These very useful reports on the reform process in different countries may be found at www.observatory.dk.

The European Health Management Association (EHMA) is an important source of information on European health management trends and has important links on its website. (www.ehma.org). EHMA has also published important comparative reviews of health policy and management, for example, in 2000, *The Impact of Market Forces on Health Systems*.

SOURCES IN SPECIFIC COUNTRIES

The comparative literature on healthcare is vast: we provide here some sources for a selected range of countries.

France

Good outlines of the French system and of recent reforms can be found in Rodwin and Sandier (1993), Duriez and Sandier (1994), Bellanger (1999), Segouin and Thayer (1999) and the European Commission (1997).

The annual reports of CREDES on the health status and social protection of the French – for example, Bocognano et al (1999), *Santé, soins et protection sociale en 1998* – constitute invaluable reference material. These are reports by the major health economic research agency on the French social insurance system. The CREDES reports provide extensive data, for example, on utilisation of health services in the social security system by different categories of those covered.

Websites devoted to the French health services include:

http://www.emploi-solidarite.gouv.fr/index.asp (Ministry of Employment and Solidarity)

www.galeriesociale.com/ese/ (*Espace Social Européen*, a website covering social security and health issues)

www.credes.fr (CREDES)

www.inserm.fr (The French Institute of Health and Medical Research)

www.cnamts.fr (The National Sickness Fund)

www.quotimed.com (*Le Quotidien du Médecin*, a medical publication)

Germany

Publications by Busse and Howorth (1999), Busse, Howorth and Schwartz (1997), Schwartz and Busse (1997) and Busse and Wismar (1997) provide valuable overviews of the German health care system and of recent issues and reforms. The WHO *HITS* (health care systems in transition) report on Germany is a very valuable source. Its website reference is http://www.observatory. dk/index-2.htm.

Other useful websites include:

http://www.statistik-bund.de/e_home.htm (Federal Statistics Office in Germany))

www.bmgesundheit.de (Federal Ministry – in German only)
www.dimdi.de (the German Institute for Medical Documentation
and Information).

United States

Stevens (1971) provides a detailed history of American medicine
up to the 1970s. O'Brien's paper (1994) gives a brief but useful
overview of the history of US healthcare in the twentieth century.
Good overviews of, or data on, a very complex system are
provided by Raffel and Raffel (1997) and Folland, Goodman and
Stano (1997). Iglehart (1999 – a and b) discusses current issues
in Medicare and Medicaid respectively. Fairfield et al (1997),
Ginzberg (1999) and Sekhri (2000) discuss current issues in
managed care.

Useful websites include
> www.dhhs.gov (the US Department of Health and Human
> Services)
> www.nih.gov (National Institutes for Health, a key research
> agency)
> www.hcfa.org (Healthcare Financing Administration, which
> administers Medicare and Medicaid)
> www.cdc.gov (Centres for Disease Control and Prevention).

United Kingdom

Levitt, Wall and Appleby (1995) provide an overview of the
system. The white papers *Working for patients* (1989) and *The
new NHS* (1997) set out the basic principles of the Conservative
and Labour government reforms respectively. Comments on the
Conservative reforms of the late 1980s and early 1990s may be
found in Appleby (1994), Ham (1997), Hatcher (1997), Le
Grand, Mays and Mulligan (1998) and Paton (1995). The NHS
Plan (NHSE, 2000a) sets out the Labour government's plans for
the services up to the year 2000. The HITS report of the WHO
(1999) on the UK is a useful source on recent reforms and is also
available online at: http://www.observatory.dk/index-2.htm.

Useful websites include
> www.doh.gov.uk (Department of Health)
> www.nice.org.uk (National Institute of Clinical Excellence)
> www.kingsfund.org.uk (The King's Fund)

www.omni.ac.uk (OMNI information gateway)
www.hsj.co.uk (Health Service Journal)
www.york.ac.uk/inst/crd/NHS (Centre for Reviews and Dissemination)
www.audit-commission.gov.uk/ (Audit Commission)
www.bmj.com *(British Medical Journal)*
www.thelancet.com *(The Lancet)*
www.jr2.ox.ac.uk:80/Bandolier/Bandolier (Evidence Based Health Care)
www.york.ac.uk/inst/crd/ehcb.htm (Effective health care bulletins)
www.soton.ac.uk/~wi/hta (Health Technology Assessment).

Canada
The HITS report of the WHO (1996) on Canada provides a useful overview of the historical development of the Canadian health services and of recent reforms (http://www.observatory.dk/index-2.htm). Other useful sources on recent issues and discussion include Leatt and Williams (1997), Lomas, Woods and Veenstra (1997; on decentralisation), Naylor (1999) and Bégin (1999).

Useful websites include:
www.healthcanada.com (Federal Department of Health)
www.cihi.ca (Canadian Institute for Health Information)
www.cihr.ca (Canadian Institutes of Health Research)
www.statcan.ca (Statistics Canada).

Chapter 4
Health Gain

INTRODUCTION

One of the key concerns for those involved in health service planning and delivery is the impact that efforts have on reducing the burden of disease and premature death on individuals and communities. Reflecting these concerns, current thinking is that the focus of health policy and planning should move beyond treatment and the delivery of services, to include measures to prevent disease or enable disease to be detected earlier where treatment is more likely to be effective. In addition, the focus has moved beyond mortality (death) to place a greater importance on morbidity (illness) and its effects on quality of life and the potential contribution of each individual within society. This expansion in thinking is reflected in terms such as 'health and social gain' and 'adding life to years and years to life' (WHO, 1995). The aim of this chapter is to outline the significance of this issue in Ireland and, drawing on the findings from the international literature, to identify some possible approaches that could be adopted to improving health and social gain in Ireland.

WHAT IS THE ISSUE IN IRELAND AND
WHY IS IT IMPORTANT?

Improving health gain is now a core aim to be found in statements relating to strategy and health policy in Ireland. However, Ireland fares poorly when health outcomes are compared to those of our European neighbours. These findings are significant especially when one considers the implications of premature mortality and poor health status on individuals and Irish society as a whole. As a nation we have a high premature mortality rate (mortality aged under sixty-five years), much of which is preventable. Irish life expectancy is still below that for most other EU countries and in 1995 Ireland had the lowest life expectancy of all fifteen countries at age 65 for both men and women. The three major causes of premature mortality in Ireland are cardiovascular disease, cancer and accidents. Chronic diseases such as cardiovascular disease, chronic respiratory disease and cancer are also major causes of morbidity in Ireland. However these figures mask, to some degree, the improvements achieved from the 1980s to the present day. These include a greater reduction in mortality rates than in most of eighteen other European countries during the 1980s, with particular improvements in premature death rates for men overall, for cerebrovascular disease, for all cancers and for accidental and violent deaths (WHO, 1998a).

There is also evidence that there are serious inequalities in health between groups and regions within Irish society. Suggesting that inequalities in health are the most pressing priority facing the health field, the Chief Medical Officer (CMO, 1999) reports that there are significant differences in mortality and chronic illness between occupational groups; sections of the population who are marginalised have poorer health outcomes; there are geographical differences and particular geographical hot spots can be identified; there are significant differences in healthy lifestyles between socio-economic groups; the less well-off in society have poorer access to health services. Further evidence of differences in health between socio-economic groups is presented in the 2001 *Health Strategy*, drawing on the work of the Institute of Public Health, Trinity College, Dublin, and the ESRI (p.31).

Yet, health gain is a key theme in current Irish health policy. The health strategy *Quality and Fairness: A Health System for You* (2001a) defines health gain.

Health gain is concerned with health status, both in terms of increases in life expectancy and in terms of improvements in the quality of life through the cure or alleviation of an illness or disability or through any other general improvement in the health of the individual or the population at whom the service is directed (Department of Health and Children, 2001a, p. 15).

This statement suggests that patients should receive clear benefits from their contact with the health system. However, as will be discussed later, health services are just one of several inter-related factors involved in health outcomes and differences between and within countries. The approaches proposed in the

Figure 4.1   Life expectancy at birth, in years

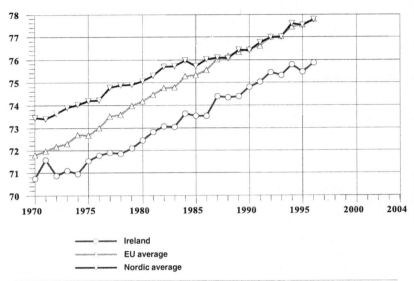

Ireland
EU average
Nordic average

Source: WHO European Region HFA Database, 1997

health strategy in 1994, to improving health gain are outlined under

- *health promotion* – refocusing the health services towards improving health status and quality of life
- *treatment and continuing care* – focusing on the role of GPs, acute hospitals and continuing care services
- *broadening the priority-setting process* – ensuring that the allocation of resources is open and objective, and that it is based on detailed information and analysis of needs, costs and outcomes.

Falling out of that strategy, a number of policy documents were launched focusing on particular areas of concern and providing national direction on approaches to address these issues, such as: the national health promotion strategy; policy documents and white papers on mental health, women's health and alcohol; and specific strategies for cancer and cardiovascular disease. The latter two strategies focus on prevention, health promotion, surveillance, screening, and evidence relating to the effectiveness of various approaches to treatment. These strategies are also reflected in regional plans. There are plans to follow a similar approach for the third biggest cause of premature mortality – accidents.

FACTORS INVOLVED IN HEALTH STATUS AND INEQUALITIES

It is now generally accepted that factors such as socio-economic circumstances, living conditions and access to and utilisation of educational services, have as important an influence on health status of a population as the provision of medical care.

> ... evidence is accumulating to show that high income and higher allocation of resources to the health sector do not automatically make for better health status. Much more attention needs to be paid to studying the underlying determinants of health, to ensuring equity in health care and to improving the quality of life (The WHO, 1994, paragraph 29).

An individual's health will also relate to other pre-disposing factors such as heredity, occupation, residence, income and behavioural factors such as diet and exercise. So complex are the factors involved in health status that behaviour may also be influenced by pre-disposing factors. For example, people on a low income may be constrained in their choice of diet and the type and amount of exercise they have. Fox and Benzeval (1995) concluded that on the basis of numerous sources of research evidence, differentials across a range of dimensions of health are related to factors such as living conditions, resources, relationships and lifestyles. These differences are to be found in all countries.

> The key point to emphasise is that across a range of dimensions of health – mortality, medically diagnosed morbidity, self-assessed objective and subjective health measurements – there is evidence of variations, whether measured by social class, housing tenure, income, car ownership, economic status or education. Such differences exist at all ages, from birth to beyond retirement, and have been found in a wide range of datasets, including official statistics, cross-sectional and longitudinal surveys and numerous small-scale studies (Fox and Benzeval, 1995, p.17).

It is important to be aware that, in addressing inequalities, spending more on health may have little impact on health outcome unless it is targeted specifically at addressing the factors influencing health and ill-health. LeGrand (1992) and Benzeval et al (1995) suggest that the availability of medical care does not have much of an impact on death rates and morbidity.

> In fact it is difficult to resist the conclusion that there is little the health service can do to reduce inequality in its use or in the private cost of that use ... rather they stem from basic social and economic inequalities ... Inequalities in health reflect inequality in society. It seems that one cannot be altered without affecting the other (LeGrand, 1992, p5).

This suggests that some of the measures aimed at improving health outcomes focused specifically on the provision of treatment services may be misdirected. For example, in Ireland the Chief Medical Officer reports that the focus of attention currently is on efficiency and issues such as waiting lists, and suggests that:

> ... in focusing the debate on this topic in the way we do, we are in fact ignoring the more fundamental and long-term issues of how we create the conditions for the promotion of long-term health and well-being in our community (CMO, 1999, p.6).

A key issue, in tackling inequalities in health, is whether inequalities can be said to be unnecessary and unavoidable such that they are judged to be unjust and unfair. Can policy measures address such issues by closing gaps between groups or societies or do they further contribute to inequalities (Daniels et al, 1998, Whitehead, 1990). For example, public immunisation programmes might have a better uptake by higher income groups than lower income groups, further widening gaps in health. Along similar lines Whitehead (1990) distinguishes differences in health outcomes that are inevitable and unavoidable, from those that are unnecessary. For example, differences arising from exposure to unhealthy, stressful living and working conditions, or inadequate access to essential health and other public services would be considered to be avoidable and unjust. On biological variations, Whitehead suggests that

> ... much of the differential between different groups in society ... cannot be accounted for on biological grounds; instead, other factors are implicated. The crucial test of whether the resulting health differences are considered unfair seems to depend to a great extent on whether people choose the situation which caused the ill health or whether it was mainly out of their direct control (Whithead ,1990, p.6).

INTERNATIONAL DEVELOPMENTS: THE ROLE OF THE WORLD HEALTH ORGANISATION

Health gain is the central theme in the World Health Organisation's (WHO) constitution (1946), which states that a fundamental human right of every human being is the enjoyment of the highest attainable standard of health. The WHO launched the *Health for All* policy in 1978 at the Alma Ata Conference to highlight the fact 'that despite the ambitious proclamations enshrined in the WHO constitution, large numbers of people and even whole countries, were not enjoying an acceptable standard of health' (WHO 1998b). One of WHO's central concerns is equity in health.

> Equity of health implies that ideally everyone should have a fair opportunity to attain their full potential and, more pragmatically, that no one should be disadvantaged from achieving this potential, if it can be avoided (WHO, 1998b).

> Equity is concerned with creating equal opportunities for health and with bringing health differentials down to the lowest level possible (Whitehead, 1995).

The World Health Organisation set a target to reduce inequalities in health between countries and within countries, by at least 25 per cent, by the year 2000. The WHO Regional Committee endorsed thirty-eight targets for the WHO European Region, relating to lifestyle, the environment and healthcare. The thirty-eight targets were revised in 1991 and again in 1998 as twenty-one targets for health in the twenty-first century (*Health21*) (see WHO,1998c). These targets are set for the European region as a whole and it is suggested that they should not be taken as equally applicable to all individual countries in the region. This acknowledges that some countries may already have achieved some of the targets, whereas others may find that targets are too ambitions.

The twenty-one targets relate to:

- *solidarity and equity for health in the European region* – reducing the present gap in health status between member states, and reducing the health gap between socio-economic groups within member states
- *improving health* – targets for better health for all new-born babies, infants and pre-school children, young people and people over sixty-five years

- *tackling specific types of ill-health* – mental health, communicable and non-communicable diseases and injury from violence and accidents
- *addressing factors influencing health* – the environment, patterns of living, harm from alcohol, drugs and tobacco, physical and social environment at home, in school, at work and in the local community, the responsibility of all sectors for health
- *the organisation of health services* – the integration of health services; the management of quality of care; the allocation of resources for health services based on equal access and cost-effectiveness; solidarity and optimum quality; human resources; ensuring that health professionals have the appropriate knowledge, attitudes and skills to protect and promote health; health research, information and communication systems to better support effective utilisation and dissemination of knowledge to support health for all; a partnership approach to promoting health; policies directed at health for all, supported by the appropriate institutional infrastructures, managerial processes and innovative leadership.

THEMES IN CURRENT NATIONAL REFORMS

Whitehead (1995) identifies four themes in international policy responses to inequalities in health

- *strengthening individuals* – aimed at individuals in disadvantaged circumstances, on the basis that 'building up a person's knowledge, motivation, competence or skills will enable them to alter their behaviour in relation to personal risk factors, or to cope better with the stresses and strains imposed by external health hazards ...'(p25)
- *strengthening communities* – their defences against health hazards, building social cohesion, and creating conditions in deprived neighbourhoods for 'community dynamics' to work
- *improving access to essential facilities and services* such as clean water, sanitation, safe and nutritious food supplies and so on
- *encouraging macroeconomic or cultural changes* to tackle poverty and wider social inequalities in society.

A range of approaches aimed at improving health gain can be identified across recent national initiatives. Attempts can be identified to devise national polices which emphasise the need to improve health overall, to address inequalities and the need for people to take responsibility for the own health. Measures are being taken to identify and explore differences in health. The factors contributing to ill health or inequalities in health are being highlighted – social and economic conditions, environmental issues and changing behaviour.

Health improvement has been a particular theme in recent policy initiatives in **Britain**. An independent enquiry into health inequalities chaired by Sir Donald Acheson in 1998 made a number of recommendations, followed by a government white paper – *Saving lives: Our Healthier Nation* (Department of Health, Great Britain, 1998) and *Reducing Health Inequalities: An Action Report* (Department of Health, 1999).   The white paper bills itself as the 'first comprehensive government plan to tackle poor health', and its central aims are to improve the health of everyone and in particular the health of those worst off.

Four themes can be identified in the document.

First, it highlights the need to tackle the social, economic and environmental factors involved in poor health, by government working in partnership with people and communities.

Second, it acknowledges that people make individual choices about their own health and can improve their own health through physical activity, better diet and quitting smoking; the *Healthy Citizens* programmes are aimed at helping people to make decisions. The three prongs of Citizens Direct are: the 24 hour NHS Direct nurse-led information and advice service; the *Health Skills* programme aimed at people helping themselves and others; and the *Expert* patients programmes to help people manage their own illnesses.

Third, it recognises that inequalities in health must be approached through a number of avenues. There is a need for government programmes aimed at employment, education, housing, neighbourhoods and the environment. Action is needed on sexual health, drugs, alcohol, food safety, water fluoridation and communicable diseases. The NHS must be re-oriented, integrating health improvement into the delivery of local health care, giving health authorities, primary care groups and primary care trusts new roles in public health. Local authorities must work in partnership with the NHS to plan for health improvement involving *Health Actions Zones* and *Health Living Centres*.

Fourth, it acknowledges that standards must be developed and success measured; this will include: the establishment of the *Health Development Agency* with responsibility for raising the standards of public health provision and a public health development fund; improved public health information and research into public health; interim milestones for the four priority areas: cancer, coronary heart disease and stroke, accidents and mental illness; local targets for improving health; performance management through the new NHS performance assessment framework.

Also in Britain, a growing emphasis on health improvement is evident in the planning cycle. Health authorities are now required to take the strategic lead in producing annual health improvement plans (HImPs). Health authorities work with local authorities and local agencies and communities to produce local plans for improving health and health services and for reducing inequalities in health (see Chapter Six, on service planning, for further information on HImPs).

The aim of health action zones (HAZs) introduced in 1997 is to address inequalities in health in areas of deprivation, through the development of locally agreed strategies for better-integrated arrangements for treatment and care. Health action zones are seven year programmes with three strategic objectives: to identify and address the public health needs of the local area; to increase the effectiveness, efficiency and responsiveness of services; to develop partnerships for improving people's health and relevant services, adding value through creating synergy between the work of different agencies (NHSE, 2000b).

Initially eleven HAZs were established in 1998 and were followed by fifteen further HAZs in 1999. Bauld and Judge's (1999) national evaluation of HAZs found that partnerships and the strategy and priorities that are developed to achieve goals were crucial to the success of HAZs.

In **Canada**, the Federal, Provincial and Territorial Advisory Committee on Population Health (ACPH) (1996) outlines a number of approaches to improving the health of Canadians. The report notes that key influences on the health of Canadians are: unemployment, child poverty, growing inequalities in earned income and certain 'worrying' lifestyle trends. Child poverty particularly affects one parent families, with infants born in low income neighbourhoods almost twice as likely to die in their first year of life as those born in high income areas. The lifestyle issues identified relate to Canadians exercising less, increasing obesity, increases in smoking among teens and high teen pregnancy rates.

Four strategy areas are proposed by the ACPH (1994) to address challenges remaining in improving the health of Canadians and ensuring that they remain 'among the healthiest people in the world'.

Living and working conditions: here the aim is to

- create a thriving and sustainable economy, with meaningful work for all
- ensure adequate income for all Canadians
- reduce the number of families living in poverty
- achieve an equitable distribution of income
- ensure healthy working conditions
- encourage life-long learning
- foster friendship and social support networks, in families and communities.

Physical environment: here the aim is to

- foster a healthy and sustainable environment for all
- ensure suitable, adequate and affordable housing
- create safe and well-designed communities.

Personal health practices and coping skills; here the aim is to

- foster healthy child development
- encourage healthy lifestyle choices.

Health services; here the aim is to

- ensure appropriate and affordable health services, accessible to all
- reduce preventable illness, injury and death.

The ACPH also notes the importance of intersectoral action and the need for good leadership to bring all the sectors together (health, finance, education, social services, housing, labour, justice, aboriginal affairs, economic development and a range of non-government organisations) to co-operate to improve health.

Health gain, in terms of improving the health status of the population and reducing inequalities in health, is the central theme in the seven principles outlined in the **New Zealand** Health Strategy as outlined in the Minister of Health's Discussion Document (Ministry of Health, 2000a). Twelve objectives are identified for immediate action. It is proposed to

- address disparities in health between Maori and Pacific peoples and other New Zealanders
- reduce smoking, improve nutrition, reduce obesity and improve the level of physical activity
- reduce the rate of suicide and suicide attempts
- minimise the harm caused by alcohol and drug use
- reduce the incidence and impact of cancer, cardiovascular disease and diabetes
- improve oral health
- reduce violence in interpersonal relationships, families, schools and communities
- ensure appropriate child health care and immunisation services.

To achieve these objectives, nine 'sector-wide' goals have been set, aimed at addressing environmental and lifestyle issues, improving physical and mental health, reducing injuries, providing more accessible and appropriate health care services, and improving the participation of Maori in the development and provision of health services.

In **Australia** in recent years, health policy has become increasingly focused on health outcomes. Key themes in policy developments are the effectiveness of health promotion activities, access to health services, and targeting particular health issues and inequalities in health outcomes between indigenous peoples and other Australians. The general approach to improving health gain involves setting goals and targets and providing guidelines and information on best practice at the national (Commonwealth) level on the one hand, and measuring health outcomes and monitoring progress made by states and territories and linking these processes into funding. Hupalo and Herden (1999) suggest that the Australian health care system, Medicare, has been instrumental in increasing access and reducing the costs for people on low incomes and that, since its introduction, Medicare has helped to narrow the gaps between rich and poor in health outcomes.

Hupalo and Herden (1999) note that one particular concern in Australia is that measures aimed at improving health do not increase inequalities in health. For example, it is well known that people on higher incomes may be more receptive to, or have better access to, health promotion campaigns, or are more likely to have the means to be able to adapt lifestyle. This concern is reflected in recent Australian Department of Health and Aged care initiatives. They aim to identify issues relating to socio-economic inequalities and health and to develop strategies to address these issues at a population area. Key elements of this work are outlined by Hupalo and Herden.

The department is developing a strategic approach to population health policy and action, focusing on the impact of broader issues on health, such as economic and social policies. This also emphasises the need for collaboration within the population health sector and the development of a partnership approach, with the department acting as facilitator and overseer. A high degree of community control is required for services to be effective and approaches need to be culturally appropriate.

Information collection systems are being developed to map, monitor and report on the burden of disease and its distribution and to explore the possible links between issues such as income on health and changes over time.

Quality and timely research is to be pursued to understand inequalities in health and to build the research networks and infrastructure.

The department also sees the need to develop effective and evidence-based population health interventions.

WHAT ARE THE LESSONS FOR IRELAND?

This review suggests that, in addition to the provision of health services and the availability of different approaches to treatment, further efforts are required to effectively address inequalities in health and to improve health status in the population as a whole. There has been a great tradition of health promotion in the Irish health system with numerous far-reaching campaigns. However, the comparative review of efforts to improve health gain suggest that a greater focus is required on the determinants of health, in terms of identifying the factors involved in poor outcomes and identifying effective approaches to addressing them. The literature from other countries suggests that material and educational deprivation (that in turn influence pre-disposition and behaviour) are probably the biggest factors influencing health. The acknowledgement that 'close and continuous inter-sectoral co-operation' is required to achieve health and social gain in the Department of Health and Children's Strategy Statement (Department of Health and Children, 1998a) suggests that the importance of a cross-sectoral approach is gaining wider acceptance. This is further endorsed in the Annual Report of the Chief Medical Officer.

> Many of the causal factors of health inequalities, such as poverty and unemployment, are outside the direct control of the health services. Inter-sectoral collaboration is required to tackle these problems, and partnership between government and the statutory and voluntary sectors is vital if the cycle of inequality is to be broken. Close co-operation between the Departments of Health and Children; Education and Science; Environment and Local Government; Social, Community and Family Affairs; Agriculture, Food and Rural Development and Finance will be required to address this important issue (Chief Medical Officer, 1999, p.31).

The National Economic and Social Council (NESC) (1999) outlines progress made on a range of approaches to addressing social and economic exclusion in Ireland over recent years. Firstly, it highlights the sustained commitment to reducing employment, such that the labour market is now buoyant. While acknowledging that unemployment is a key factor involved in social exclusion, it also points out that unemployment is not the only factor and that poverty, educational deprivation and housing status are also important factors in Ireland. It describes the changed Irish society compared to that in the 1960s as one that is younger, better educated, more urbanised, with increased female participation in the workplace and society, and one that is more open to change. However, it suggests that despite recent economic success, serious problems still remain, some of which are 'now starker against the transformed background' and that economic success also brings with it new challenges. Most notably, marked inequalities still exist, relative income poverty is still high by EU standards and has increased over the period from 1987 to 1997. In addition, the proportion of gross national product (GNP)(after adjustment) spent on social protection is below the EU average. Yet social protection is one mechanism through which inequalities can be addressed.

Following on from the Chief Medical Officer's (CMO) Report in 1999, where the need to identify and address the inequalities that currently exist in Ireland is a key theme, the Office of the CMO's annual report in 2000 focuses on the health of Ireland's children. Child health as a central theme in this second report from the CMO is seen as being particularly timely, following closely on the heels of the National Children's Strategy (Department of Health and Children, 2000c), aimed at enhancing the status and quality of life of children in Ireland. The focus on child health is also promoted as a strategic approach to enhancing the longer-term health and well-being of Irish people. It provides an analysis of child health status, child health services, and broader socio-economic determinants of child health. It recommends that 'specific policy measures which redistribute resources, provide opportunities and services for families with children, especially poor children, will do most to create better child health' (p.7). In addition, it recommends that a broad range of interventions relating to income, family support, child care, and education and health services to support children's health are required.

The importance of the partnership approach to addressing these sort of cross-cutting issues (issues that cut across the remits of more than one government department or sector) is now well recognised across countries (see Boyle, 1999). Social inclusion, poverty and social protection are key themes in the work carried out by NESC, which itself is made up from representatives nominated by government, business and employers' organisations, the Irish Congress of Trade Unions, agricultural and farming organisations and the community and voluntary organisations. The 1996 NESC report promoted the importance of a multi-faceted and integrated response to these issues. In addition, the National Anti-poverty Strategy, a joint commitment between the social partners, government and NESC (1999), suggests that it is likely to be successful in enhancing progress over the next few years. The 2001 Health Strategy recognises the importance of factors such as socio-economic, cultural and environmental factors, and community networks on the health of individuals. Accordingly, one of the stated aims of the strategy is to 'ensure that health is given priority across all the sectors with a role to play in improving health status' (p. 16). One of the functions of the new Population Health Division, to be established in the department, will be to conduct health impact awareness/health proofing of policies proposed, including those initiated outside of the health sector.

Health surveillance is also an important aspect of approaches to be found in other administrations. In Ireland, work on developing a public health information system (PHIS) began in 1995 with a national survey providing the baseline data for a public health minimum dataset. Originally, the focus in PHIS was on mortality rates. The emphasis currently is on developing more composite measures of public health. *Shaping a Healthier Future* (1994) outlined an explicit role for directors of public health within health boards to monitor and report on health status across health board area populations. In line with this move, small area statistics focusing on differences in disease patterns within health boards are being developed to complement the PHIS data. The 2001 strategy also proposes to enhance this role further by developing population health functions in the health boards. These will work closely with the Population Health Division in the department. It is anticipated that the PHIS database, along with the on-going work on public health measurement within health boards, will allow longer-term health outcomes to be monitored year-on-year and inequalities between and within health boards to be identified and addressed. Currently, the PHIS contains data on three types of population health outcomes – fertility, mortality and morbidity. A small amount of data is also kept on outcomes of care – caesarean sections, low birth weight and causes of mortality. It is anticipated that the PHIS and national cancer register will enable progress on longer-term health outcomes to be monitored at national and regional levels in the future and for closer examination of inequalities in health across the country. The inclusion of data on cardiovascular disease and other health outcomes in time, and further development of small area statistics, will enable inequalities within and between regions to be identified and used as a basis for specific strategies to target inequalities.

Further, as seen in the comparative review of approaches taken in other countries, there is increasing emphasis on screening and early detection of disease. Cervical and breast screening services are not yet available in all health boards areas, but a number of pilot schemes are in place and the plan is to extend them to all health board areas in time. Elements of screening and early detection are also to be found in the national cancer and cardiovascular strategies, emphasising the importance of integrated approaches to improving health gain.

This review has identified a number of other broad community-based approaches that could be developed in Ireland, such as workforce-based health promotion and prevention initiatives, to create a healthy environment and health action zones along the lines of those in the UK. The World Health Organisation launched its *Health Promoting Hospitals* network in 1988, aimed at developing health promoting projects and programmes at hospital level; enhancing communication, co-operation and exchange between participating hospitals; sharing programmes to make better use of resources; identifying areas of common interest to develop programmes and evaluation procedures; and identifying examples of good practice to be shared. Projects can be selected from six areas: the well being of patients and staff; co-ordination of primary care and hospitals; prevention; health education and rehabilitation; sanitation and protection of the environment; and the relationship between the community and social institutions. The network was established in Ireland in 1997 and in 1999 (Midland Health Board, 1999) it was reported that fifty-three hospitals in Ireland were participating in the scheme.

The 2001 *Health Strategy* also highlights the need to provide individuals with the information and support they need to make informed choices and that will enable them to take greater responsibility for their own health and well-being.

Chapter 5
The Public-Private Mix

INTRODUCTION

What is the appropriate mix between the public and private sectors in health care? What services should be funded by the state? What services should be funded privately? How should links between public and private hospital care be organised? How should private health insurance be regulated? Most health care systems, including our own, are grappling with these very complicated questions. In 2001, a major *Irish Times* series (O'Sullivan, K., 2001) contrasted Ireland's public-private mix with what it saw as the most equitable arrangements in many other OECD countries.

Definitions and classifications in this area are very complex. Writing in a Canadian context, Deber et al (1997) highlight the importance of *financing* (how services are paid for); *delivery* (how services are provided to recipients of care); and *allocation* (how resources flow from those who finance care to those who deliver it – though they add that this is more an issue of the degree of government control and of reimbursement incentives than a public/private issue).

In Ireland, major changes have taken place in private health care and private insurance in recent decades and thus in the public-private mix. Following an EU directive, competition was introduced to the private health insurance market in Ireland in 1994. A major government white paper on private health insurance – the first major government policy statement on this area – was published in 1999. Considerable debate has also taken place about the links between public and private care and about inequities of access between public and private patients.

This chapter will look at some current issues in the Irish public-private mix and at possible lessons to be learnt from an examination of policy developments in other countries such as Australia and Germany. As this is a vast area of policy, the coverage of the chapter will necessarily be selective. The focus will be on issues related to private health insurance and to access to care of public and private patients.

WHAT IS THE ISSUE IN IRELAND AND WHY IS IT IMPORTANT?

A striking feature of the Irish health services is the rapid growth in the numbers of those with private health insurance. According to the White Paper on Private Health Insurance (Department of Health and Children, 1999c), the number of those with private health insurance coverage has increased from 22 per cent in 1979 to 42 per cent in 1999. Private funding has also increased as a percentage of total funding, from around 18 per cent in 1980 to 23 per cent in 1996.

Competition was introduced into the private health insurance market in 1994. The British United Provident Association (BUPA) entered the market in 1997 as a competitor to the Voluntary Health Insurance Board. Much debate has since taken place on the principles (such as community rating) and structures (such as risk equalisation mechanisms) which should underpin such competition. The 1999 white paper, *Private Health Insurance*, announced decisions on some of these key issues. This document and policy surrounding private health insurance will be analysed later in this chapter.

Policy debate has taken place on the extent to which the state subsidises the private system – for example through tax relief for private health insurance premiums – but most criticism has focused on the perceived preferential access of private patients to acute hospital care. This chapter will first examine these issues in the Irish context before considering international trends

RECENT DEVELOPMENTS AND DEBATES IN IRELAND

Overview of developments in private health insurance
In 1953, eligibility for free hospital services was extended to around 85 per cent of the population. The VHI was established by the state in 1957 to provide private health insurance (PHI) to the remaining 15 per cent of the population which did not enjoy such eligibility. This chapter has already outlined the steady growth from the 1970s in the numbers of those in Ireland with PHI coverage.

Significant changes in the private health insurance environment took place in the 1990s. The Health Insurance Act 1994 came into effect on 1 July 1994. It was designed to allow for competition and to regulate the Irish private health insurance market on foot of the Third EU Directive on Non-Life Insurance. Although it required competition in the health insurance market, the EU directive accepted the need for regulation in that market, in the interests of the common good. In compliance with this directive, the Health Insurance Act of 1994 permitted other health insurance companies to enter the Irish health insurance market and thus ended the monopoly of the VHI.

The operation of market forces in private health insurance is subject to Irish government regulation. In the 1994 Act, and in subsequent regulations in 1996 under the Act, the government set out key principles which all insurers must accept. These include community rating, open enrolment and lifetime cover. Community rating means that the same premium rate must apply to all adult persons having a particular level of cover, whatever their age, sex or health status. Community rating is influenced by concepts of equity and incorporates the principle of 'inter-generational solidarity' which ensures that people of a different age do not pay different amounts and more specifically that the old do not pay more than the young. In the words of Durkan (1998), 'community rating sets premia based on the risk charac-teristics of the entire membership of the scheme, and involves cross-subsidisation from low-risk to high-risk groups' (p.55).

Open enrolment means that registered health insurance companies cannot refuse health insurance cover to a person under the age of sixty-five except in certain limited circumstances. Lifetime cover means that once a person is insured with a registered undertaking, the insurer cannot terminate or refuse to renew the contract except in certain limited circumstances. The legislation also requires each insurer to offer a package of minimum benefits – incorporating the equivalent of semi-private cover in a public hospital. The legislation also provides for risk equalisation – a scheme designed to prevent 'cherry picking' which occurs when insurers target low risk groups to the exclusion of high risk groups.

Following on the legislation and regulations, a Risk Equalisation Scheme was established in Ireland in 1996 in order to make transfers, where necessary, between insurers with the aim of equalising their 'risk profiles' (the types of patients who insure with them) and thus of supporting community rating. The scheme sought to ensure that it would not be possible for any insurance company to benefit (by paying out less in patient claims) from targeting lower-risk or younger patients. The thinking was that if this happened, the community rating basis of the Irish system would be undermined. Any competitor wishing to survive would also be obliged to target lower risk customers and in time elderly patients would pay more than the young.

Debate about health insurance policy and about the application of market principles to the health insurance sector has focused on community rating and risk equalisation. After the establishment of competition, the British company BUPA entered the Irish market (from January 1997) and has been engaged in competition since with the VHI. BUPA has argued that regulations here favour the VHI (which continues to enjoy a fairly dominant position in Irish health insurance) and amount to a restriction on competition. BUPA has thus opposed the risk equalisation scheme established in 1996. The VHI's view is that without such a scheme of risk equalisation, it would be impossible to preserve the principle of community rating, an important principle of Irish health policy.

In its submission to an Advisory Group on Risk Equalisation, which reported in April 1998, BUPA argued strongly that a risk equalisation scheme was not necessary and that normal market forces could be relied on to ensure that different insurers do not obtain very different risk profiles. The Report of the Advisory Group (Department of Health and Children, 1998b) took the view however that risk equalisation was essential to underpin community rating. In late 1998, the government decided that the existing risk equalisation scheme would be changed and that BUPA-Ireland would not have to make the payments to the risk equalisation fund for which it was liable under the existing risk equalisation scheme.

The 1999 white paper also referred to the establishment of a Health Insurance Authority for which the Health Insurance Act, 1994 had provided; the appointment of its first members were announced in March 2001 by the Minister for Health and Children. The white paper retained in a somewhat modified form both community rating and a risk equalisation mechanism. Thus the government announced proposals to introduce lifetime community rating – meaning that insurers will have the discretion to apply or to waive late entry premium loadings as their business needs and plans require. Thus a sixty-year old who has been in the private health insurance system for twenty years might pay a lower premium than someone of the same age who has just joined the system. The white paper also announced some adjustments to the risk equalisation mechanism: the government, it stated, was committed to implement a risk equalisation system incorporating some elements of a casemix approach. This risk equalisation system had not been introduced by early 2002 but is expected to be set up during 2002 under regulations governed by the Health Insurance (Amendment) Act, 2001. The Health Insurance Authority will have a good deal of discretion in advising on when risk equalisation between insurers should be initiated.

In a comment on the Irish health insurance regulations, the OECD (1997) made a positive judgement about what might be called their 'equity dimension':

> They ensure the continued availability of the current type of cover and are aimed at preventing individuals from being under-insured due to lack of proper understanding of the restrictions which might apply to some types of policies. In addition, they will maintain the current level of inter-generational solidarity ... Some of the regulations, such as those relating to minimum coverage, seem unnecessary on consumer protection grounds, as there is now a universal public hospital service, but may be justified by the need to have an adequate spread of risk to allow community rating to work. Others, such as not relating premia to age, may be justified on equity grounds and the need to minimise the extent to which the elderly population use the public system (pp.149-150).

Public-private inequities
The 1999 white paper drew attention to some state incentives and supports which ensure that private health insurance has remained an attractive option: for example, tax relief on health insurance premiums and the maintenance of public hospital charges for services to private patients at a level below the economic cost. Some have argued that these measures constitute an unacceptable level of subsidy of private health insurance by the state.

On the other hand, the white paper maintained that :

A case can be made in favour of some level of state incentive to the individual to effect private health insurance, on the basis that those who opt for private cover effectively forgo a statutory entitlement while continuing to contribute to the funding of the public health service through taxation (p. 24).

It is possible to argue, in other words, that private patients pay twice for hospital care – through taxes and private insurance premiums.

Public discussion has however highlighted a perceived preferential treatment of private patients. In relation to the costs of private care in public hospitals, the white paper noted that the government would be commissioning research in this area. That research was published in October 2000 in an ESRI report, *Private Practice in Irish Public Hospitals* (Nolan and Wiley, 2000). This report found that private patients in public hospitals were being substantially subsidised by the state. The study found that public hospitals recouped only half of the cost of caring for private patients from insurance companies, with the taxpayer making up the shortfall. Admission through accident and emergency departments was, the report suggested, the main reason that private patients were sometimes accommodated in public beds.

In a general critique of the public private mix in Ireland, Wren (2000) argued on October 2 in an *Irish Times* series that 'the state is moving rapidly towards an American-style system where people's ability to pay delivers access to care'. She argued that there were 'deep-seated inequities and irrationalities' in the present system and that the 'vested interests of some medical professionals' (specifically the private practice incomes of hospital consultants) was taking precedence over patients' needs (2000, p. 13).

Somewhat similar arguments have been advanced by an academic commentator, Durkan (1998). According to him, what health insurance in Ireland provides is faster access to health services, a faster access which should be seen in the context of the dual public and private role of many of the agents in the system:

Public hospitals have public and private beds, hospital consultants can have public and private patients, and can function out of more than one hospital, and in public and private hospitals (p. 54).

Durkan argues that the system gives both the hospital consultant and the public hospital an incentive to lengthen waiting lists among public patients. One could argue that the government has also benefited from an expansion of PHI. From a government point of view, a strong performance by the VHI has had cost containment spin-offs in the public health system. Durkan argues that 'in periods when public health expenditure was curtailed, there was a tendency for VHI membership to rise' (p.54). One might also relate the growth of private health insurance to an increased affluence in Ireland since the late 1970s.

Another academic commentator, Kinsella (2001), also highlighted inequities in the system and argued for a shift in the health burden from the public sector. He made a case for compulsory private health insurance in Ireland, though without spelling out in detail how this might work in practice.

The debate on perceived public-private inequities has now led to political proposals for reform. In a statement accompanying the launch of the Labour Party policy document, *Curing Our Ills*, in April 2000, the party spokesperson, Liz McManus TD, stated: 'At present Ireland has a two-tier health system which is based on a form of apartheid that is fundamentally unfair and inefficient. Our health hospital system is grounded on the 'ability to pay' principle. It provides rapid access to non-emergency hospital services for those with the financial means to get care and long queues for those who rely on public services' (McManus, 2000).

The Labour Party envisaged an extended role for the state in the form of free GP services to all and the provision of 800-1000 new consultants – what it called a move from a consultant-led to a specialist-provided service. It argued that the best way to progress was not to eliminate the advantages given by private health insurance but to ensure that these advantages were extended to all by the introduction of a universal health (hospital) insurance scheme. The state would pay 100 per cent of the insurance cost for those with incomes below a specified threshold.

In November 2000, the Fine Gael policy document on health, argued that:

In today's Ireland, if you can pay you will live longer and in less pain, while those on low incomes must suffer on. This is unjust, unacceptable, and untenable and runs counter to the principles of Fine Gael, a party that is part of the European Christian Democratic tradition (Fine Gael, 2000).

The document stated that Fine Gael proposed to end the two-tier system in public hospitals by introducing a universal insurance-based system funded through the exchequer.

Prior to the adoption of the *2001 Health Strategy*, the Fianna Fáil-Progressive Democrat government had given priority to expanding access to, and investment in, the public health services, for example, through extending medical card coverage to those over seventy, through the increased capital investment provided for in the National Development Plan and through sustained efforts to reducing waiting lists in the public hospital system. As well as providing for significant additional resources for investment in out-patient and accident and emergency services and hospital beds, the 2001 strategy introduced guarantees on waiting times for public patients and stated that any new beds in the public hospital system would be reserved for public patients. The strategy also indicated that services for public patients could be purchased in private hospitals; it announced that a new Treatment Purchase Fund would be used for the sole purpose of purchasing treatment for public patients who had waited more than three months from their out-patient appointment.

Controversy has also surrounded the relationship in Ireland between public and private provision in long-term care. A report by the Ombudsman in January 2001 (Office of the Ombudsman, 2001) was very critical of the operation of the system of payment by health boards of subsidies or subventions to patients in private nursing homes as provided for in the Health (Nursing Homes) Act, 1990. The report maintained that the department and the health boards did not properly implement the law which obliged them to subsidise private nursing home care where public care is not available.

Somewhat in contrast to criticism of inequities in the Irish system, *The World Health Report 2000* of the World Health Organisation scored Ireland highly on 'fairness of financial contribution' in an international comparison of health systems. The measurement was based on the fraction of a household's capacity to spend (income minus food expenditure) that goes on health care (including tax payments, social insurance, private insurance and out of pocket payments). Ireland's community-rated premiums for private health insurance and the country's provision of entirely free health care to the most needy clearly influenced Ireland's high placing in this international classification. Though there might be significant inequities in the delivery of care here, the WHO was clearly suggesting that financing of care was relatively equitable in Ireland. This WHO report included a league table of world health systems based on criteria such as overall level of health, fairness of financial contribution, distribution of health in the population and responsiveness.

INTERNATIONAL TRENDS

Any analysis of comparative healthcare literature quickly reveals that most developed countries are grappling with complex issues in relation to the public-private mix which are similar in many respects to those faced in Ireland. Writing in a Canadian context, Deber et al (1997) state:

> The issue is not whether the system will be 'public' or 'private' in the future, since virtually every country employs some public/private combination in various sectors of the health system. Rather a number of options exist for balancing the public-private mix (p. 2).

In **Australia**, according to Banks (1999), the private insurance industry accounts for 10 per cent of Australia's total healthcare spending and 20 per cent of hospital funding. There has been considerable Irish interest in Australia, partly because of some policy similarities (for example, the support for community rating in both countries) and partly because of the severe problems faced by the Australian private insurance system in the 1990s. Serious affordability problems developed in Australian PHI, including a 'vicious circle' of falling membership, premiums rising as payouts rose; lower risk members dropping out as PHI became more expensive; and a riskier and smaller pool of PHI members being left so that average payouts rose. Banks states that by 1996, barely a third of the Australian population had some form of PHI, as opposed to about one half almost a decade before (p. 7).

In **France**, the social insurance system provides coverage to almost the entire population, but Segouin and Thayer (1999) point out that there has been recent debate about access issues, for example for those (such as the homeless) who are not covered by social insurance and therefore risk falling through the net. The introduction in 1999 of the Universal Medical Coverage system, which simplifies access to the system, was designed to respond to the problems of such people. There is also debate about the problems caused by co-payments for those on modest incomes and about the income levels at which co-payments should be waived. Levels of co-payments are relatively high and most French people (an estimated 85 per cent of the population) therefore have supplementary health insurance to cover their co-payment costs. Supplementary private health insurance is thus an important part of the French system.

Bellanger (1999) notes that French patients enjoy a choice of provider among generalist and specialist doctors working outside the hospital; and also enjoy significant choice in access to public and private hospitals. She states that freedom of choice gives patients a greater arbitration role, which leads to competition between physicians. Nevertheless, she adds, the competition is limited because of patients' lack of information.

The **German** system is a 'Bismarckian' system (see Chapter 2) which currently covers almost 90 per cent of the population (according to Busse, 1999). Sickness fund membership is compulsory for employees whose gross income is below a certain limit and voluntary for those above that limit. Nine per cent of the population is covered by private health insurance and 2 per cent by free governmental health care (for example, soldiers). In 1997, according to Busse, 56 per cent of hospital beds were public, 38 per cent not-for-profit and 6 per cent were private.

Debate on reform in Germany has focused not on differences between public and private care but on reform within the public health system. For example, Busse (1999) considers the implications of the free choice of sickness funds for insured persons. He argues that if the choice is to operate properly, then sickness funds need to be able to contract with providers and that a risk compensation mechanism is needed if competition is to operate properly. His analysis of reform requirements related to the publicly funded system rather than (as might be the case in Ireland) to difficulties of interaction between public and private care.

Traditionally, in **Britain**, the NHS was dominant in healthcare provision and the private acute hospital sector was marginal but that sector and the number of those with private health insurance has grown in recent decades. Doyle and Bull (2000) state that around 12 per cent of the population now have private medical insurance (clearly, a much lower figure than in Ireland) while 34 per cent of long-term care for elderly people is provided privately.

A question of definition in international debate is whether private health insurance (PHI) is complementary or supplementary. Banks (1999) says that PHI has a complementary role where it provides an alternative to public funding and provision and a supplementary role where it is simply funding optional extras of comfort or choice in the context of a universal health system. The Irish PHI system, which covers close to half the population for all their acute hospital expenses, may be seen as a system which is complementary, rather than merely supplementary, to the public system; while the French system, which largely covers co-payments under a universal social insurance scheme, may be seen as supplementary. Private health insurance may be seen as supplementary rather than complementary in Britain.

Saltman, Figueras and Sakellarides (1998) note that in countries such as Germany and the **Netherlands**, private health insurance is the only form of risk pooling available to, or availed of, by part of the population – for example, 9 per cent of the population in Germany. Governments in Germany and the Netherlands have tried to provide social protection for such persons through regulation. The Netherlands developed in 1986, for example, a policy position similar to that in Ireland in relation to open enrolment and risk equalisation. Under this policy:

> All private insurers are required to provide open enrolment into a standard package policy (SPP). An equalisation system allows some transfer of resources among the private insurance funds to cover high-risk cases (Saltman, Figueras and Sakellarides, 1998)

Private insurance may thus be seen as complementary rather than merely supplementary in Germany and the Netherlands.

In his reflection on the Australian system, Banks (1999) argues that if a system is merely supplementary, then risk rating is appropriate; but if it is alternative or complementary to public funding and provision, then regulations to ensure equity (such as community rating) are required.

Another theme in the international literature has been the importance of stability in the market. The sharp drop over a short period in Australian private insurance coverage is seen as a worrying example of the real possibilities of instability.

One of the solutions recommended by the Australian Productivity Commission (1997) to the country's PHI problems was the introduction of lifetime community rating, which penalises late entry into PHI and thus encourages early entry and lifetime cover. The Irish white paper of 1999 also announced the introduction of lifetime community rating to Ireland.

Irish policy makers and health insurance companies have debated community versus risk rating in recent years, as well as the mechanisms needed to support community rating. Both sides of the argument have reflected on the lessons of international experience, including that (for example) of Australia or the US.

The VHI has stressed the need for a risk equalisation scheme to support community rating. The VHI (2000) has highlighted the difference between Irish conditions and those pertaining elsewhere in Europe:

About 45 per cent of the population are privately insured compared to between 12 per cent and 15 per cent in other European countries where the market is risk rated (p. 2). It adds:

Community rating makes it possible for people to afford effective health insurance throughout their lives. Ireland's community-rated market has 45 per cent market penetration for health insurance while the risk-rated UK market with four major health insurers has only 12 per cent penetration (p. 3).

The VHI notes that community rating underpinned by a form of risk equalisation operates in Israel, Holland, Australia, the German Sickness Funds, Belgium, South Africa and certain US States.

This defence of community rating is supported by Light (1998), who reviews the US experience. In the **United States**, after World War II, commercial insurers were allowed to risk rate alongside the community-rated policies of the existing companies: Blue Cross (which covered hospital expenses) and Blue Shield (which covered doctors' fees). According to Light (1998), the policy lesson of this experience is that once risk and experience rating begins, it undermines community rating: 'To have an 'open market' in which both approaches exist is to spell the end of community rating'. Light adds that risk rating by age was followed by risk rating by disease and by specific medical or genetic risks.

BUPA (2000), which highlights the importance of competition in PHI, does not accept that comparisons with countries such as the US or Australia are appropriate. It argues that Ireland ought to be compared instead with other EU countries such as the UK, Sweden, Denmark and Spain which have a 'universal national health system, funded through general taxation, and where people can obtain private insurance on top of the state systems' (p.4). BUPA (2000) argues that 'the international evidence does not prove the assertion that risk equalisation is necessary for community rating' (p.5).

However, official policy in Ireland to date has consistently held that risk equalisation is necessary for community rating. As noted, the 1999 white paper, having reviewed the evidence, including the report of an Advisory Committee in 1998, decided that a modified risk equalisation system was required:

> The Government believe that risk equalisation is compatible with a competitive insurance market. Furthermore, they are of the view that a risk equalisation system is an essential feature of a health insurance market where insurers are required to operate on a community rating/open enrolment basis (par. 4.9, p. 42).

As noted earlier, however, the introduction of this risk equalisation system – a cause of great controversy between the VHI and BUPA – is now expected in the course of 2002.

If the VHI-BUPA debate has focused on the requirements for fair competition, Schneider (1999), writing from an Australian perspective, argues that competition between health insurers is a relatively minor aspect of health care financing. If we are to ensure PHI is affordable for a large section of the population, he argues, we need to ensure more competition between the providers of health care : the doctors and hospitals.

WHAT ARE THE LESSONS FOR IRELAND?

Any analysis of the public-private mix raises many complex issues and international experience is difficult to summarise – every system is grappling with complex problems including the challenges posed (in OECD countries) by ageing populations.

Proposed solutions are clearly influenced by varying political or philosophical perspectives, particularly perspectives on the role of the state in healthcare and of the private sector.

The first obvious lesson from a review of international experience is that most countries have some form of public-private mix in health care. The co-existence of public and private practice is not unique to Ireland. In France, for example, around two thirds of doctors are private practitioners and most of them provide publicly funded services. Private provision is also extremely significant in countries such as Germany and the Netherlands.

Writing in a Canadian context, where there is guaranteed public funding of essential care but much private provision, Deber et al (February 1997) state:

> The issue is not whether the system will be 'public' or 'private' in the future since virtually every country employs some public-private combination in various sectors of the health system. Rather, a number of options exist for balancing the 'public-private mix' (p. 2).

Writing in a New Zealand context, Scott (1998) expresses similar sentiments:

> The current 'mixed' system ... is likely to continue into the future ... the debate should explore the best assignment of roles, responsibilities and interfaces across the two sectors (p.1).

Views inevitably differ a good deal on the type of 'mixed' system which works best but Deber et al (February 1997) make a strong case for public financing for medically necessary services (even if the definition of medical necessity has posed problems in the Canadian context).

A second basic lesson from comparative study is that the public-private inequities which are causing great controversy in Ireland do not appear to exist to the same degree in several other OECD countries – for example, France or Britain. There are some differences in coverage between Ireland and these other countries, but equity differences seem to result from a clearer separation in those countries than in Ireland between public and private care rather than from any differences in coverage per se: in Ireland, there is now universal coverage in the acute hospital sector, even if free GP care is available only to the poorest third of the population.

As FitzGerald (2001) has argued, an important cause of Irish inequities would appear to be the interaction of public and private care in the health services; this interaction, he suggests, has led to inequality between public and private patients in access to acute hospital care: for example, a much quicker access of private patients to out-patient appointments.

If there are significant problems in the public-private mix in Ireland, it should be acknowledged that other countries are also grappling with significant problems in the funding (whether public or private) of health care and in the delivery of care. One might point here to perceived problems of under-funding or of lengthy waiting lists in the UK or to cost containment pressures in France or Germany. Thus the British NHS Plan (NHSE, 2000a) announced that the government would be increasing spending in Britain to bring it closer to EU levels. A lengthy French commentary on the social security system there (Wenz-Dumas, 2000) made no reference to public-private issues in France but focused in great detail on cost containment difficulties and challenges in the public system since the Juppé reforms of the mid-1990s. German health policy makers have accorded great priority to cost containment since the 1970s.

If there has been justified criticism of public-private inequities in Ireland, there are no simple answers to the policy issues here or elsewhere. In Ireland, the extension of free health care (or more specifically of free GP care, as acute hospital care was already available free of charge) to the entire population along the lines of the British NHS has sometimes been seen as the solution to our access or equity problems; but the NHS model has itself been subject to serious strain – in Britain itself in recent years, the involvement of the private sector has been growing rather than diminishing.

Irish interest has also grown in the experience of countries such as France, where there is fast access to hospital care for virtually all patients irrespective of income or social class and where the health services have benefited traditionally from generous funding levels. In France, however, policy makers have placed great emphasis since the mid-1990s on cost containment and there are also concerns about the implications of an ageing population structure for future health care funding

If the introduction of continental-type social insurance systems has sometimes been suggested as the solution to inequities in Ireland, both the Commission on Health Funding in 1989 and the *White Paper on Private Health Insurance* (Department of Health and Children, 1999c) were opposed to going in that direction. The white paper argued that such a change:

> ... would require a radical overhaul of the current healthcare and health insurance systems which would incur significant costs. The government considers that the resources which this process would demand would be better used for the improvement of the public healthcare system (p. 18).

The 1999 *White Paper on Private Health Insurance* included few specific references to international experience but its recommendations were clearly based on a sustained Irish reflection on that experience, including developments in countries such as Australia. The white paper referred specifically to demographic trends in other EU countries and to the healthcare challenges posed by ageing populations.

Although it recommended some changes to, and highlighted some problems in, the Irish private health insurance system (PHI), the white paper's analysis of the Irish public-private mix was relatively positive. Thus it referred in some detail to the OECD (1997) review of the Irish healthcare system, which concluded that Ireland had achieved a good provision of healthcare at relatively low cost to the taxpayer.

The white paper also set out some of the detailed positive findings of the OECD. Private health insurance (PHI) has tried to ensure that many people stay in the PHI system, thus relieving the cost of hospital care to the public finances. Working in public hospitals remains attractive to consultants. PHI premiums do not vary with age, making it more likely that older people stay in the system.

Some other findings of the OECD (as reported by the white paper) relate however to significant public-private inequities or ambiguities in Ireland. Thus the OECD recommended that: the commitments of consultants to both the public and private sectors need to be better defined; charges for the use of public hospital facilities should be put on a more economic basis; the impact of competition should be carefully monitored, so as to avoid high-risk groups being pushed back into the public sector with adverse consequences on health expenditure.

These OECD findings may be seen in a sense as the broad policy framework within which the 1999 white paper operated and which the Irish government therefore accepted on the basis of the reflection, during the white paper process, on international experience of the public-private mix.

There is clearly now a new emphasis in Irish debate on equal or at least comparable access to health care for public and private patients. This emphasis has been influenced by a perception of excellent access to health care on the part of almost all citizens in many other European countries.

Public policy here has advocated not the abolition of the public-private mix or of private care in public hospitals, but rather increased investment in public care. In 2001, the report of the Forum on Medical Manpower (Department of Health and Children, 2001b) highlighted the importance of equity in hospital provision: 'While a mix of public and private hospital services is recognised as government policy, it is important that principles of justice and equity remain central to the delivery of patient care' (par. 5.3).

Some of the recommended changes (which again are influenced by a perception of generous health care funding in other countries) require increases in health care funding. Thus the changes envisaged by the Forum on Medical Manpower (Department of Health and Children, 2001c) included significant increases in consultant numbers in the public hospital system. Equally, the National Task Force on Medical Manpower was set up in 2001 to examine the resource implications of increased consultant numbers and of reduced working hours for non-consultant hospital doctors.

Chapter 6
Service Planning

INTRODUCTION

The accountability legislation – the Health (Amendment) (No 3) Act (1996) – sets out the requirement for health boards to submit a service plan to the Department of Health and Children each year. In it, health boards are required to outline the services to be provided for the year, along with estimates of income and expenditure. The legislation also sets out a specific timeframe within which the service plan is to be adopted and approved by the health board, and states specifically that the implementation of the service plan is the responsibility of health board chief executive officers.

WHAT IS THE ISSUE IN IRELAND AND WHY IS IT IMPORTANT?

Since 1996, the service plan has become a critical component of the accountability framework in terms of ensuring the provision of appropriate, effective and equitable services and the effective control of resources. The preparation of annual service plans is seen as a means of establishing the principles of strategic management in health boards and a central component of enhancing accountability (Dixon and Baker, 1996). Dixon and Baker also suggest that service plans could become a key feature of organisational performance review, providing an opportunity to integrate programme objectives and to cascade resulting performance requirements down to units or departments. The first service plans were produced in 1997 and health boards have been developing their approach to service planning significantly over the last few years.

Butler and Boyle (2000), in their review of service planning in Ireland, suggest that the production of the annual service plan needs to be seen in the context of a strategic approach to service

72

planning overall. This view positions the service plan as a key link between the strategic and the operational, translating strategic objectives into priorities and objectives for the year, which can then be cascaded down to managers and staff in operational plans. In this sense, the requirement to produce an annual service plan provides the opportunity for health boards to review the board's progress against longer-term strategies in the light of changes that have occurred during the year.

As a legal document, the service plan provides evidence that the board is meeting its objectives and demonstrates that services are the result of sound planning and reflect national and local policy. The service plan also has an important part to play in monitoring and evaluation, by providing the benchmark against which the performance of health boards and health providers can be demonstrated. Once the service plan is accepted by the department, it provides the basis on which the performance of the health board is monitored. An initial set of performance indicators has been agreed for inclusion in the service plans for 2000.

INTERNATIONAL DEVELOPMENTS: SERVICE PLANNING IN ENGLAND AND NEW ZEALAND

The framework for service planning in England and New Zealand is not unlike that in Ireland, the main differences being the relationship between purchasers and providers and payments at the point of delivery. The two countries are used here firstly because of their comparability with Ireland in terms of their planning frameworks, and secondly based on the availability of up-to-date information on service planning. In both countries a purchaser/provider split has been pursued over recent years aimed at enhancing accountability. More recently, the emphasis on competition between providers has been replaced with an emphasis on co-operation. Both systems are now built around devolution of responsibility for planning within a set regulatory framework. This approach is aimed at shifting the focus from inputs to outputs, thus providing an emphasis on results while leaving room for innovation. In England, recent developments are also aimed at matching national priorities for health improvement with local needs for health and personal social services. The following key elements of service planning can be identified in both systems.

Central strategic direction

In both systems there is evidence of strategic direction from the centre. In New Zealand, the Ministry of Health provides the strategic direction for the development of health services. It receives advice from the independent National Health Committee on national priorities. Each year policy guidelines – including national priorities – are issued by the ministry to the Health Funding Authority (HFA). In 2001, the HFA was subsumed into the Ministry of Health and twenty-three District Health Boards (DHBs) were established to fund and manage integrated care for each of their catchment areas. The thinking behind this integration is that the new arrangements will provide the best prospects for the government's objectives in health and disability to be met, and will help to 'retain an overview of the sector, to align policy and funding decisions nationally and services at the level of the consumer' (Ministry of Health, 2000b, 2000c). Transitional arrangements are currently in place, but from 1 July 2002, DHBs are expected to be fully functional (Minister of Health, Annette King, 2000). The New Zealand Health Strategy (Ministry of Health, 2000c) identifies twelve objectives to be adopted nationally and to be reflected within accountability arrangements between the Ministry of Health and the DHBs. Based on these and local needs, DHBs will be required to produce district annual plans, which will incorporate the funding agreement and the statement of intent and will be agreed with the Minister of Health (Ministry of Health, 2001).

In England, the role of the National Health Service Executive (NHSE) is to provide clear strategic leadership to health authorities and NHS trusts, to enable them to secure the greatest possible improvement in physical and mental health through the resources available. Its leadership role is to provide the strategic framework for health service development, to disseminate knowledge and information and to manage the NHS to ensure that national policy is implemented. Each year the NHSE plan sets out an overview of the external factors affecting demand and their likely impact on services and describes in-year priorities for the NHS, thus contributing year-on-year to longer-term strategy and key objectives. NHS priorities and planning guidance are issued to health authorities (HAs) and the NHSE's business plans draw on the annual NHSE plan.

Recent reforms in England are also aimed at the centre and regions working more closely together in balancing national and local priorities. Health authorities (HAs) are required to submit service and financial frameworks (SFFs) to the NHSE regional offices before performance agreements are drawn up between the NHSE and the HA. The SFFs provide the link between local and national priorities and between immediate and longer-term priorities. They take into account anticipated allocations and require wide consultation with professionals and the public. According to the NHSE (1997), the SFF has a role in securing early decisions on the broad framework for the year and in settling any strategic issues in good time, in order to ensure time to resolve the detailed issues on service agreements with providers in a constructive manner. The SFF, once received, will be evaluated by the NHSE regional office to ensure that it is consistent with national priorities and targets and is acceptable as the basis of corporate contracts between the HA and the NHSE regional office:

> (The SFF) should provide all parties with a clear overview of the services planned for the health authority population in (the year), the resources available for them and the priorities that will be followed if it proves necessary to modify plans to reflect changing circumstances (NHSE, 1997, p.5).

Locality planning

In New Zealand, the newly established DHBs are expected to balance the needs of local communities with national frameworks, encouraging equity and consistent prioritisation between competing demands. This is a role that was previously carried out through locality planning by the HFA (Health Funding Authority, 1999). DHBs will be required to draw up district strategic plans, which will cover a period of five to ten years, be based on an assessment of the health status and health service needs of the population for which it is responsible, and involve consultation with the population at draft stage. District annual plans will outline services to be funded for each locality, drawing on district strategic plans.

The recent requirement of health authorities in England (1999/2000) to produce health improvement programmes (HImPs) is aimed at providing a bottom-up approach to strategic planning, to complement the central strategic direction provided by the NHSE. HImPs are to provide a shared statement of local response to national priorities and targets. HImPs are based on the health authority's assessment of local needs, working with primary care groups, NHS trusts, local authorities and other local interest groups and include action plans to address issues raised.

Allocating resources on the basis of assessed need
Needs assessment is an important element of service planning, to enable services to be targeted at the needs of populations and towards achieving health and social gain. In New Zealand resource allocation between localities is based on the population-based funding formula (PBFF), which takes account not only of the size of the population but of some of the key health-related characteristics of each population. The New Zealand Public Health and Disability Act (2000) established the DHBs to improve, promote and protect the health of the people and communities in their regions. In addition, DHBs will be responsible for funding most health services in their regions, either directly or through funding other providers. The Act also requires DHBs to assess the needs of their populations for services, to provide a basis for funding decisions and as a key input into strategic and annual plans (Ministry of Health, 2000d). Health policy specifically identifies the need to tackle known disparities between Maori and non-Maori health outcomes.

In England, funding is allocated to districts on the basis of weighted capitation aimed at ensuring equity in the distribution of services. The formulae used are based on the *Resource Allocation Working Party* (RAWP) formula developed in 1979, which was modified considerably in 1990 and again in 1995. Allocations made to each health authority are published annually. More recently the introduction of health actions zones is aimed at a cross-cutting approach to reducing known inequalities in health by targeting particular geographical hot spots.

Moves towards longer-term funding arrangements
Service planning in the two countries, as is the case in Ireland, involves an annual planning/purchasing cycle between the centre and regions, within a wider strategic framework. In order to provide greater flexibility in service planning, longer-term arrangements are being put in place between funders and providers.

In England, longer-term agreements are currently being introduced between HAs and providers on a phased basis. Their introduction is aimed at reducing bureaucracy and refocusing clinical and management effort on quality and cost-effectiveness. They are directed at reflecting longer-term arrangements between HAs, primary care groups and NHS trusts and on developing a shared view of the outcomes of care needed.

In New Zealand, the range of contracts that would have existed between the HFA and providers included annual contracts, multi-annual contracts and contracts set up as and when needs or opportunities arise during the year. Initially, it is proposed that DHBs will have 'largely prescriptive funding' arrangements in place, but that in time, there will be greater opportunities for increased flexibility (Ministry of Health, 2000c).

Clear monitoring and accountability arrangements
Monitoring and evaluation are important features of service planning to ensure that allocated funding is used to provide appropriate and effective health services. In both countries reviewed, health planning is based around devolution of responsibility for planning to decision makers at regional level within an explicit regulatory / accountability framework. The accountability frameworks include specific lines of accountability and funding pathways. That is, the DHBs/health authorities are responsible for monitoring the performance of providers and the DHBs/health authorities in turn are monitored by the ministry /NHSE, with whom they have funding/ management agreements.

In addition, there are regular formal arrangements for reporting and the return of management information to demonstrate performance. The key accountability document between the Ministry of Health and the DHBs is the funding agreement which contains a number of performance measures and a service coverage schedule. DHBs are required to report on financial and non-financial performance monthly and quarterly to the Minister of Health. DHBs are also required to submit an annual report to the Minister of Health to be tabled to parliament, which outlines the DHB's performance against budgets and performance measures set out in its statement of intent. The New Zealand Public Health and Disability Act (2000) requires DHBs to monitor the performance of service providers and detailed guidance has been issued by the Ministry of Health to DHBs. DHBs are required to put in place service agreements with providers stipulating the quality, access to, and amount of services required.

In England, health authorities are required to provide central data returns on a monthly, quarterly or annual basis. Required data is generally organised into datasets and standardised as central returns. Data collected centrally is reviewed every three years to assess its current value in the light of the cost of collection. Also, in England, health authorities are required to publish an annual report describing performance over the previous year, an annual report to the Director of Public Health, and an annual report on performance against Patient's Charter rights and standards. Health authorities are also required to publish a five-year strategy document and are required to make available, on request, annual purchasing plans and contracts with providers. England and New Zealand are also among a number of countries moving towards the development of national performance indicator systems.

WHAT ARE THE LESSONS FOR IRELAND?

Four major issues are highlighted by a comparison of service planning in Ireland, England and New Zealand. The first relates to the requirement in Ireland to produce annual service plans within a strategic approach to service planning. This is not unlike the approaches in England and New Zealand where an annual purchasing/funding round of negotiations and agreement takes place within a strategic framework. A top-down approach is taken in New Zealand where national priorities are identified by the independent National Health Committee and disseminated by the Minister of Health to DHBs. In England, recent reforms are aimed at providing both a top-down and bottom-up approach to identifying strategic priorities. Butler and Boyle (2000) suggest that the link between service planning and strategic planning needs to be strengthened in Ireland, so that the service plan becomes a vehicle to move strategy forward and for health boards and providers to achieve and revise objectives.

Secondly, locality planning is aimed at balancing local priorities with national priorities in planning services and developing a shared response amongst health service providers to health needs in a region. This is reflected in formula-based approaches to resource allocation. Butler and Boyle also suggest that the service planning process in Ireland needs to be more clearly focused on increasing health and social gain within populations and tackling inequalities in health both between and within regions. This will require considerable development in needs assessment and in matching resources to differences in assessed needs.

The third key point relates to the centre and regions working more closely together at key stages in the planning process to allow key priorities to be matched with resource allocation. As shown in this review, arrangements for service planning in England allow the priorities for service provision to be agreed before funding is allocated. However, it is not clear from the literature how well allocations reflect priorities identified for the year.

The fourth key point raised relates to monitoring in the service planning process. As shown, there are clear arrangements in both systems for monitoring between the centre and purchasers and between purchasers and providers. The approach includes clear lines of accountability, the requirement to produce annual reports, to make other planning documents available on request and to return data on performance. However, it is not clear from the literature on service planning in England and New Zealand how required returns and reports reflect the key objectives outlined in planning documents – as opposed to centrally set targets and indicators. The need to enhance the evaluation and monitoring aspect of service planning in the Irish system was identified by Butler and Boyle (2000).

Chapter 7
Developing Performance Measurement

INTRODUCTION

Across health systems, there is a growing awareness of the potential that performance measurement has; in enabling national priorities for health reform to be translated into organisational and individual objectives; in refocusing energies on achieving results; in enhancing accountability; and in enabling decision making about services to occur close to where they are delivered. This comparative review focuses on approaches taken across five countries – Canada, the US, Australia, New Zealand and Britain – to developing performance measurement. It also focuses on concepts of performance and measures used in performance frameworks.

WHAT IS THE ISSUE IN IRELAND AND WHY IS IT IMPORTANT?

In Ireland, a number of recent national strategy and policy documents and legislative changes highlight the need to develop effective performance measurement systems in the health sector. The role of the Department of Health and Children is becoming increasingly focused on policy development and overall control of expenditure, with the explicit devolution of its current role in operational management to executive agencies. The purpose of devolution is to enable decisions to be made closer to those who use services, thus enabling services to be more responsive to the needs of users. It will also enable the department to focus explicitly on its role of providing national oversight of the health system, on health planning and policy, and on issues of national interest. For effective devolution in the health sector, performance measurement systems are required. These can enable health boards and providers to demonstrate that they are fulfilling devolved responsibilities and allow the department to monitor the performance of the system against agreed objectives.

As identified in *Shaping a Healthier Future* (1994), performance measurement is also required to demonstrate effectiveness and value for money to the taxpayer and to focus services on specific goals and targets. High performance is one of the four goals of the 2001 *Health Strategy*. This will include the development of a strategic, evidence-based approach to management and enhancing accountability. The need to enhance accountability in the health services was identified by Dixon and Baker (1996). It is also endorsed by recent changes in legislation, the *Public Service Management Act* (1997), the *Comptroller and Auditor General (Amendment) Act* (1993), and the *Health (Amendment) (No 3) Act* (1996).

The Department of Health and Children's strategy statement document for 1998 suggests that performance measurement in the Irish health system is intended to:

- encourage the attainment of the highest standards of effectiveness, efficiency, equity, quality and value for money in the health delivery system
- strengthen accountability at all levels of the health service, and
- optimise staff performance, training and development (Department of Health and Children, 1998, p.8).

INTERNATIONAL DEVELOPMENTS

A comparative review across a number of countries shows that the development of performance measurement is a high priority for most countries.

The emphasis in **Australia** is on defining national performance standards, developing performance measures and making performance data available to decision and policy makers at all levels (Australian Government Publishing Service, 1996). Performance measurement features strongly in the funding cycle in the Australian health care system. Health care agreements (HCAs) between the Department of Health and Family Services and the eight states/territories explicitly require states/territories to report and share information on a regular basis. It also requires states/territories to contribute to the development of national performance indicators with a particular focus on health outputs and outcomes. The emphasis currently in Australia is clearly on acute health care. The National Health Minister's Benchmarking

Working Group (NHMBWG) is working on the development of performance indicators (PIs) in the acute care hospital services sector because information is more readily available in this sector and the use of PIs is more developed. The Australian Council on Healthcare Standards (ACHS), in collaboration with the specialist medical colleges, is developing sets of clinical indicators for use in the ACHS accreditation programmes of acute healthcare providers. The National Hospitals Outcomes Program commissioned Boyce et al (1997) to examine the range of performance indicators being developed in various health systems and in Australia. They were asked to identify possible indicators of quality of health care and health outcome for use in a national indicator set for acute health care in Australia.

In **New Zealand**, the funding agreement between the Ministry of Health and the Health Funding Authority (HFA)/ District Health Boards (DHBs are expected to be fully functional from 1 July 2002) is the key accountability document between the centre and regions. Performance expectations are outlined in funding agreements; these must be aligned with the Crown Statement of Objectives, the statement of national priorities for the year. Clear monitoring requirements are outlined in the funding agreement, including the requirement of the HFA to submit quarterly reports and to report on progress against agreed key deadlines. The funding agreement also requires information to be returned on a monthly basis, which is largely based around activity. In addition to monitoring arrangements outlined in the funding agreement, the HFA has selected ten national integrated care demonstration projects for the development of a collaborative framework for health service providers. Each project is focused on health outcomes and has clear objectives and targets against which progress will be measured. Once DHBs are fully established, they will be required to provide monthly and quarterly reports on financial and non-financial performance to the Ministry of Health and to produce an annual report on performance against budgets and performance measures included in its annual statement of intent. Both the statement of intent and the annual report are to be submitted to parliament.

The current National Health Service (NHS) reforms in **Britain** are focused on providing responsive, high quality and better-integrated services aimed at reducing inequalities in health and improving the health of the population. *A First Class Service*

(NHSE, 1998) outlines a three-pronged approach to improving performance. It proposed that national standards be set and service models be defined, providing guidance and audit on best practice. Clinical governance was envisaged to ensure that standards are delivered. The introduction of the NHS Performance Assessment Framework (PAF) would be aimed at monitoring service delivery. The establishment of the Commission for Health Improvement was seen as underpinning the emphasis on quality. The Commission would be responsible for local reviews of services to ensure that systems are in place to monitor, assure and improve quality. An annual national survey of patient and user experience would provide feedback from users on quality issues to be addressed.

A set of high-level performance indicators was introduced into the system in 1999. The Department of Health's Clinical Accountability and System Performance Evaluation research group (CASPE) is also developing sets of performance indicators for ten common conditions.

Performance measurement in the US has not been driven from the centre to the same extent as in any of the three previous examples. It is built primarily around the accreditation of health care organisations. The thinking is that providers will be under pressure from users and health plans to seek accreditation in order to demonstrate the quality of the services that they provide. There are two key players in accreditation in the American health system. The Joint Commission on Accreditation of Healthcare Organisations (JCAHO) accredits a range of acute, ambulatory and community-type health care organisations. The National Committee for Quality Assurance (NCQA) accredits health plans and Health Maintenance Organisations (HMOs). Both organisations carry out their own on-site evaluations towards accreditation, and while the NCQA has developed its own set of performance measures, the approach taken by the JCAHO is to provide guidance for organisations to select their own performance measurement systems.

In 1999 the JCAHO announced the establishment of a collaborative agreement with the NCQA and the American Medical Accreditation Program (AMAP - the American Medical Association's organisation for the accreditation of physicians) designed to ensure the co-ordination of performance measurement activities across the entire health system.

Consequently, the establishment of the Performance Measurement Coordinating Council (PMCC) is aimed at reducing duplication, co-ordinating the development of universal measures, standardising data requirements for different systems, improving data quality and developing guidelines for the appropriate use of performance data. It is believed that this form of collaboration will also help to reduce the costs of data collection and reporting.

In **Canada**, the Canadian Institute for Health Information (CIHI, 1998) was set up in 1993 to ensure the co-ordinated development of a comprehensive and integrated health system for Canada, with specific responsibility for health standards development and gathering, processing and disseminating health information. In addition, the National Forum on Health, established in 1994, identified the need for better tools to assess population health and for the development of evidence-based decision making supported by an improved IT infrastructure. In 1997, the federal government allocated $50 million towards the development of a Canadian Health Information System (CHIN). CIHI identifies a number of performance measurement systems being developed at the national level:

- a national health surveillance system to co-ordinate and share information on public health among 400 to 500 institutions, linked with disease prevention and health promotion
- a National Population Health Survey conducted by Statistics Canada which produces quarterly reports on population health statistics
- HEALNet/RELAIS, a national network of researchers, where the focus is on evidence-based decision support systems, including performance indicators for health care organisations and practitioners
- the Partnership for Health Informatics/Telematics aimed, at the 'creation of a non-redundant, non-conflicting set of health informatics and telematics standards for Canada' (CIHI, 1999).

At the provincial/territorial level, the shift to community-integrated health service delivery models is supported by the development of information systems to integrate and link dispersed care providers, managers and policy makers. The aim is also to improve information sharing and develop outcome measures, best practice guidelines and accountability. Within each province/territory there are a number of initiatives focused on developing information systems and performance measurement.

KEY THEMES ACROSS COUNTRIES IN THE DEVELOPMENT OF PERFORMANCE MEASUREMENT SYSTEMS

Across systems a number of themes can be identified relating to the development of performance measurement systems. These are outlined in Figure 7.1.

At the national level, there are a number of examples of governments defining national priorities and standards, which are cascaded to regions and organisations to inform the development of service provision.

The second approach seen across countries relates to promoting change and building managerial capacity. This might include putting in place mechanisms to ensure the compliance of organisations, for example through legislation or through requirements in funding contracts. Softer approaches would include the introduction of incentives that focus the attention of organisations on developing performance measurement. Another approach is to sell the need for performance measurement by promoting it as a priority area in strategy and policy documents.

A third approach at the national level is the development and introduction of a national assessment framework. Such frameworks enable progress to be monitored at a national level, perhaps against national standards, and also between and within regions.

At the organisational level, examples of efforts to develop performance measurement include accreditation, comparative analysis with similar organisations, benchmarking and clinical governance.

Performance indicators

Currently, a considerable emphasis is being placed internationally on the development of performance indicators. Terms such as quality indicators or outcome indicators are sometimes used interchangeably with performance indicators. The important point to be made about performance indicators is that they are just that – indicators of the performance of a system rather than

Figure 7.1   Approaches to developing performance
measurement

At the national level

➢ Defining the performance required
   • clarifying national priorities
   • defining standards of performance required
   • developing service models

➢ Providing the impetus for change
   • promoting the development of performance measurement
     through national strategy and policy documents
   • building performance measures, reporting and monitoring on
     funding arrangements and contracts
   • introducing legislation to enhance accountability and health
     service performance
   • supporting organisations to improve and measure
     performance
   • providing incentives to change

➢ Developing assessment frameworks
   • population health surveillance
   • generic performance assessment frameworks
   • condition/service-specific data sets

At the organisation level

➢ Accreditation
➢ Comparative analysis and benchmarking
➢ Clinical governance

enabling any judgement to be made on the quality of care. This
is reflected in the following definition:

> Indicators: Statistics or other units of information which
> reflect, directly or indirectly, the performance of the
> healthcare system in maintaining or increasing the well-
> being of its target population (Boyce et al, 1997).

Comparisons between organisations (external comparisons)
or internal comparisons, say between current performance and
that in the previous year, can be used to raise issues for closer
examination. For example, a hospital with a comparatively high
Caesarean section rate may at first appear to be a cause for
concern. However, closer examination could reveal that as a

specialist unit it attracts a higher proportion of women with complicated pregnancies, which is consistent with the higher proportion of women having Caesarean sections.

The NHS Performance Assessment Framework being developed currently in **Britain** will initially feature a set of high-level performance indicators, intended not as direct measures of quality but to flag issues for further investigation. Later it is anticipated that more detailed and comprehensive indicators will be developed with a particular emphasis on quality, cost-effectiveness and improvements in health. The aim of the high level performance indicators is to encourage benchmarking between health authorities, trusts and primary care groups and to provide accessible information for clinicians and managers when comparing their own performance and identifying good practice 'beacon organisations'. They are also intended to enhance statutory and service accountability. Also in Britain, the CASPE research group is developing health outcome indicators for ten conditions.

In **Australia** the Australian Council on Healthcare Standards' Care Evaluation Programme is the major programme underway for acute quality indicators. Currently, there are about sixteen indicator sets in use for accreditation programmes. In the **US**, several organisations are involved in the development of performance indicators, such as the JCAHO Indicator Management system; the NCQA Health Employer Data and Information Set; the Maryland Hospital Association Quality Indicator Project; Consortium Research on Indicators of System Performance (CRISP); and a number of others.

Sheldon (1998) suggests that the emergence of performance indicators is the result of 'new public management' requiring organisations and people to be accountable and to set down benchmarks for the legitimacy of organisational action. He suggests that the use of performance indicators could lead to unwanted side effects. There is the danger of an emphasis on negative rather than positive aspects of performance. Existing effective though informal quality promoting activities may be upstaged and current values could be replaced by 'abstract managerial values'. He warns against possible dysfunctional side effects such as fear and feelings of loss of control by professionals, inappropriate use and reporting of indicators and an over-emphasis on measurement, neglecting curiosity and learning.

Based on his interpretation of international experience with performance indicators, Sheldon recommends caution. He recommends that the use of performance indicators should be integrated and co-ordinated with other approaches to quality improvement such as evidence-based practice. He also suggests that indicators are more likely to be useful at local level, where there is an understanding of the underlying processes, than at national level. He believes that the use of performance indicators should be used to create trust and participation.

There are two striking findings from a comparative review across health systems. First, efforts are focused predominantly at the system/national and regional/organisational levels of the system. This suggests that the focus now needs to move to performance measurement at the individual level and to a link in with performance management. Second, the focus in many systems tends to have been on acute services, although increasing interest is expressed in looking at other health care settings, in exploring integrated health care models and in building systems around health care outcomes and improvements in population health.

COMPARING IRELAND AND OTHER COUNTRIES.

Current approaches to performance measurement in the Irish health service are outlined in Figure 7.2. As identified in other systems, the development of performance measurement in Ireland has focused on the national and organisational levels with little attention to the individual level. In addition, performance measurement is most developed in the acute sector. The Public Health Information System (PHIS) database is a public health minimum dataset set up in 1995. Within health boards, departments of public health are developing small area statistics, focusing on differences in disease patterns within health boards to complement the PHIS data. It is anticipated that the collection of public health data through these approaches will allow longer-term health outcomes to be monitored year-on-year and inequalities between and within health boards to be identified and addressed.

An initial set of performance indicators was agreed for inclusion in service plans in 2000 and will be built on year-on-year. Monthly integrated management returns (IMRs) are also

Figure 7.2:   Performance measurement in the
                   Irish health system

System	Level	Focus
Public Health Information System (PHIS)	National, health board and agency	Public health
Strategy indicators e.g. anti-cancer strategy	National and health board	Specific conditions/programmes
Performance indicators (service plan and minimum data sets)	Health board	Service plan objectives, benchmarking
Integrated Management Returns (IMRs)	Health board and agency	Finance, HR, activity, commentary
Hospital in-patient system (HIPE)	Agency (acute hospital only) and aggregate for health board	In-patient activity/case mix

Source: Butler (2000)

used to monitor performance against the service plan and are required from health boards and voluntary hospitals. The main function of the IMRs is to enable the finance unit in the Department of Health and Children to monitor and control expenditure and staff numbers across the health sector against allocations set out in the letter of determination at the beginning of each year. Some basic activity data is also included.

At the national level, a number of sectoral/programme-related data suites are being developed. The most advanced of these systems is the hospital inpatient enquiry (HIPE) database. HIPE data is the basis of casemix analysis and health boards have access to information on their own performance and national performance overall. Datasets are also being developed for programmes/areas such as mental health services, intellectual disability services and physical disability services.

Exploring understandings of performance across systems

To unwrap the meaning of performance in health services, a useful exercise is to compare concepts of performance and the types of measures used to capture performance across different health systems. Then, by comparing the findings with what is happening in the Irish system, gaps and issues to be addressed can be identified. Our comparative review looked at performance measurement frameworks in the United States, HEDIS 2000 developed by the National Committee for Quality Assurance (NCQA, 1998); Canada, the POPULIS framework developed by the Manitoba Centre for Health Policy and Evaluation (MCHPE, 1999); Australia, a framework proposed by Boyce et al (1997); and Britain, the NHS Performance Assessment Framework (NHSE, 1999). Across the four frameworks, six key concepts can be identified: health improvement/outcomes; effectiveness and quality; patient-orientated services; access; financial/resource management; and supporting indicators.

Similar concepts of performance are to be found across the Irish health service, although coverage is patchy and the most comprehensive and balanced sets are to be found in acute services. However, the concept of 'patient-orientated services' is not explicitly included in performance measures currently in the Irish system.

Comparing concepts of performance with those found in the Irish health system

In the case of health improvement/outcomes, the focus in Canada and Britain is on premature/standardised mortality and life expectancy; disease specific deaths; suicide and accidents; and on standardised morbidity.

In Ireland, population health outcomes – fertility, mortality and morbidity – are included in the Public Health Information System (PHIS). Health outcomes for cancer are recorded on the National Cancer Register. It is anticipated that further development of the PHIS will enable progress on longer-term outcomes and inequalities in health across the country to be monitored more effectively.

When we looked at measures relating to effectiveness/quality we identified a focus on effectiveness but also on appropriateness.

Three concepts of effectiveness are to be found across the four frameworks. Firstly, measures of outcomes of care such as composite measures of premature deaths and avoidable mortality, clinical outcomes, self-reported outcomes and adverse events/ complications. Secondly, there are retrospective indicators of ineffective care, such as potentially avoidable hospitalisation, mortality and readmission rates within thirty days of discharge, emergency psychiatric readmissions and dental decay in five year olds. The third type of measure found relates to safety and technical proficiency.

In the Irish system, measures of effectiveness include increased uptake of immunisation, breast feeding, paediatric surveillance and use of foster carers; quality improvement/ monitoring systems; cases subject to audit in acute hospitals; initiatives to evaluate the quality of services and client satisfaction; ongoing staff training; and indicators of adverse quality – readmission rates in mental health services and the number of complaints received in acute hospitals.

Two types of measures of appropriateness can be found in frameworks. Firstly there are measures relating to the use of treatments, which on the basis of research evidence are now known to be effective, or, as their effectiveness has not been demonstrated, are now thought to be inappropriate. Secondly there are measures of prevention and early detection of disease, for example, vaccination, breast and cervical screening, chlamydia screening, prenatal care in first trimester and postnatal check-ups.

Appropriateness of treatments is measured in several ways. The NHS PAF has measures for coronary artery bypass graft, PTCA (percutaneous transluminal coronary angioplasty), and hip replacement rates – treatments known to be effective when used appropriately. In addition, the NHS PAF also includes measures for treatments now considered to be inappropriate such as D&Cs in women under forty years of age and the use of grommets for glue ear. Other measures of inappropriate care include hospital admission for conditions amenable to good medical treatment in the community, or that are avoidable with good medical care, in other words, that with good medical care would probably not have necessitated hospital admission. There are also proxy indicators for population-based differences in particular interventions; and, measures relating to what is considered to be good practice such as controlling blood pressure, appropriate medications for asthma and comprehensive diabetes care.

Measures used to track appropriateness in the Irish system include: re-attendances in accident and emergency departments and outpatient departments; the rate of transfer of inpatients in mental health services where treatment in the community is more appropriate; data on length of stay, discharge destination and number of day cases by diagnosis related group (DRG) recorded on the hospital inpatient enquiry system (HIPE).

Across frameworks, measures relating to the patient orientation of services include measures of patient focus – responsiveness, waiting times and accessibility, skill, care and continuity; measures of patient perception – satisfaction, acceptability, and the physical environment, organisation and courtesy of services; and measures of consultation – involvement, information and choice. As previously stated this is an area for particular attention in the Irish system. The *Programme for Prosperity and Fairness* (2000) suggests that measures should be developed relating to extended hours of service, reduction of waiting times, audits of patient satisfaction and improved communication.

Two types of indicators relating to access can be found across the four frameworks. The first type relates to the distribution of services and includes access to elective surgery, inpatient services, dental services, breast and cervical screening, primary care practitioners, nursing homes and the supply and use of beds. The second type of access indicators relate to the quality of access, such as the availability of interpretation services, waiting times for elective surgery, outpatient appointments, the emergency department and emergency admission.

In the Irish system, measures of the distribution of services found include the proportion of older people assessed as requiring services who actually receive them within a certain timeframe and the proportion of targeted school children covered by dental screening. Measures of quality of access include waiting times for outpatient appointments and inpatient admissions, and waiting times in outpatient and emergency departments.

Measures of financial/resource management across frameworks include the cost of care, efficiency and indicators of health plan stability. In the Irish system measures of resource management are used in the integrated management returns (IMRs) and include expenditure, income, employment and variance against agreed budgets. Efficiency indicators are only used in three areas – child/family services, environmental healh and food control areas.

Supporting indicators are found in the Canadian framework – POPULIS. These include socio-economic risk characteristics and measures of demographic changes. These indicators make it possible to make sense of data recorded on health outcomes. In the Irish system, data on age and sex is recorded in the PHIS system to enable population profiles to be analysed. Measures were also found in service plans that relate to the implementation of good practice, such as protocols for GP referral or the implementation of strategic objectives.

Comparing measures and indicators of performance
Different types of measures/indicators are also used to capture data across six concept categories:

a) *Rates*, used in relation to mortality, low birth weight, day cases, suicide, and immunisation, for example. Rates may be expressed per 1,000 or in more complex measures such as standardised mortality rates (SMR).

b) Measures of central tendency such as *averages, means* or *medians* are used, for example, average length of stay, average waiting times, and average number of decayed, missing or filled teeth in five-year-olds. POPULIS uses median length of waiting times and the NHS PAF uses a casemix adjustment for length of stay.

c) Different measures can be used to express performance against demand, needs or good practice. *Proportions* can be used to measure performance in terms of expressed demand, for example the proportion (percentage) of members of a health plan receiving mental health or chemical dependency services. Proportions can also be set out against standards of expected practice, for example the patients seen within thirteen weeks of GP referral; the proportion of prescribing that is generic or patients on waiting lists for twelve months or more. Proportions can also be expressed against the total number with assessed needs, against target groups, or against a defined standard. Ratios may also be used to express performance against expected practice, for example, the number of recall to new attendances in outpatients departments.

d) *Costs*: the NHS PAF uses adjusted unit costs for maternity and mental health services. DRGs are used in the HEDIS system and Boyce et al (1997) propose measuring costs per casemix-adjusted separation. Although not yet included as performance measures, work is going on in the Irish acute sector to develop costing data related to DRGs.

e) *Composite measures*: the NHS PAF uses a number of composite measures to assess an element of performance by more than one measure. For example, one measure of the effectiveness of care is a composite of age standardised rates for five procedures. To assess the health outcomes of NHS care, one measure is a composite, age standardised measure of readmission rates and rates of surgery interventions for hernia recurrence.

f) *Other measures of performance*: other types of indicators of performance are used such as patient surveys or case by case analysis, indexes based on several measures or descriptive measures, for example the health plan descriptive information in the HEDIS system. Measures may also be related to objectives to be achieved, such as particular strategies or recommendations.

The types of measures most used in the Irish health system are measures of central tendency and particular initiatives to be achieved, such as the establishment of a particular service. Proportions and ratios are also used but as suggested by Butler (2000), measures could be better linked to population needs and progressive achievement. For example, a target for the provision of so many extra places in a service area needs to be set out against the number of places that would be required to meet the needs of the local population. This comparative review also highlights some possible ways in which the type of measures used to capture health service performance could be developed in the Irish system. One example is the development of composite measures aimed at providing a more comprehensive view of a particular issue.

WHAT ARE THE LESSONS FOR IRELAND?

In reviewing approaches to developing performance measurement in Ireland, a number of similarities can be seen with what is happening across other countries. Our comparative review suggests the following priority issues for the development of performance measures:

- extending performance measurement beyond national and organisational levels to include the individual level

- extending performance measurement beyond acute hospital areas to include community and other non-acute or hospital areas
- developing a more comprehensive and balanced set of performance indicators across all service areas and developing more sophisticated measures
- developing integrated data management systems to ensure:
  - relevant performance data is available throughout the system to those who need it, which is timely and in the appropriate format for analysis and interpretation
  - the reliability and comparability of data, and
  - the compatibility of data management systems
- developing managerial capacity and promoting the use of performance data as a key management tool
- co-ordination and collaboration in the development of management systems to ensure a coherent approach and to encourage benchmarking and sharing of good practice.

Chapter 8
Quality Management
in Healthcare

INTRODUCTION

The aim of this chapter is to consider quality in health services, to reflect on the growing international interest in quality and to look at possible approaches to improving quality. The chapter examines common themes in quality management and considers several possible approaches in the Irish context. It highlights at the outset some of the difficulties involved in defining what we mean by good quality health services.

WHAT IS THE ISSUE IN IRELAND AND WHY IS IT IMPORTANT?

Quality of care is one of the core principles underpinning the 2001 Health Strategy: *Quality and Fairness: A Health System for You*. It is aimed at delivering the highest quality of care and support to all people. It states that:

A quality outlook must underpin the planning, management and delivery of services within the health system. Quality can then be measured and demonstrated in an objective way (p.86).

Leahy (1998a, p.152) suggests the health strategy provides central policy direction in a system where the approach to quality management previously was 'sporadic and individually driven'. Leahy (1998b, p.107) states that 'movement towards a widespread quality culture in the Irish health care system is compelling and irreversible'. He suggests that with the growing emphasis in health care on accountability, and in the light of increasing patient expectations, quality will have to be seen to be delivered.

DEFINING QUALITY

In broadest terms, quality can be defined as the ability to satisfy 'all those features of a product (or service) which are required by the customer' (ISO, 2001). *Shaping a Healthier Future* (1994) refers to two aspects of quality 1) technical quality – that the quality of treatment must result in the best possible outcome, and 2) the consumer's perception of quality – referring to the efficiency of services, the courtesy shown and physical surroundings experienced by those using the system. Traditional concepts of quality, where the emphasis is on the fitness of a service or product for specification and reducing variation between products, are of limited value in healthcare. Health services need to be fit for purpose and their quality will be judged on how they enable the diverse needs of individuals to be met in a responsive and seamless way and on how the limited resources available for the delivery of health services are put to best use. As suggested by Doherty (1991):

> ... in our system the aim of quality should be to do the greatest good, for the greatest number of people, with the amount of resources available.

Moss (1998) alludes to some of the difficulties in conceptualising quality in health services:

> Good quality health care is so much more than a measure of the technical aspects of clinical interventions. Much of health care is a series of compromises and trade-offs and choices made in the best circumstances by fully informed patients guided by knowledgeable health professionals in appropriate surroundings. Good quality care also incorporates appropriate and technical care with opportunities for patients to make choices and to discuss concerns and anxieties, and it should result in an outcome appropriate to the problem. Even this long and cumbersome description excludes some of the important aspects of good quality health care, such as fairness and access, and assumes much in the phrase 'competent technical care' (Moss 1998, p.73).

Other concepts included in quality health care are effectiveness, social acceptability, efficiency, availability, relevance and equity (Leahy, 1998a). Further, Klein (1998) suggested that it is probably best to think of quality in terms of a 'shorthand for defining good performance'. Emphasising the need to recognise the number of different perspectives to quality among the range of stakeholders involved in health, Ovretveit (1991) defines quality from the perspectives of clients, professionals and managers (Figure 8.1). This definition reflects the different understandings that various stakeholders can have of the concept of quality in health services.

Figure 8.1:   The three dimensions of health service quality

Client Quality
What clients and carers want from the service (individuals and populations)

Professional quality
Whether the service meets needs as defined by professional providers and referrers, and whether it correctly carries out techniques and procedures which are believed to be necessary to meet client needs

Management Quality
The most efficient and productive use of resources, within limits and directives set by higher authorities/purchasers

---

Source: Ovretveit (1991, p4)

MANAGING QUALITY

A range of terms, such as quality assurance (QA), total quality management (TQM) and continuous quality improvement (CQI), is used to describe approaches to quality management. The emphasis in TQM and CQI is on designing quality into services rather than on retrospective inspection, a key element in quality assurance. TQM focuses on building a quality culture so that everyone is working to the same quality agenda.

TQM is an approach to improving the effectiveness and flexibility of a business as a whole. It is essentially a way of organising and involving the whole organisation, every department, every activity, and every single person at every level. For an organisation to be truly effective, every part of it must work properly together, recognising that every person and every activity affects, and in turn is affected by, others (Oakland, 1989, p.14).

The emphasis in CQI is on continuous assessment of an organisation's efforts, to monitor and improve the quality of services and ongoing evaluation in order to ensure satisfactory outcomes. In this sense, CQI helps to address a common criticism of quality approaches, that quality reviews are retrospective rather than continuous. Leahy (1998a) suggests that the CQI approach may address fears that quality improvement – like consumerism – benefits the middle-class consumer most, neglecting wider issues relating to the overall population, as it examines processes for all and therefore it benefits all current (and potential) users of the service. According to Colton (1997) the CQI approach is emerging as the dominant approach, internationally, to evaluation in healthcare organisations.

INTERNATIONAL TRENDS

A common concern across countries is that the cost of health care should be balanced with the quality of care received, consumer satisfaction and universal access to at least a minimum level of care. Furthermore, it is generally accepted that targeting resources to provide appropriate and effective care is also likely to result in cost savings. In addition, the profile of quality management has been raised due to growing public expectations based on an increased awareness and knowledge of health issues and their rights to a good standard of health care. The increased emphasis in the health sector on quality of care also reflects the increased emphasis on assessment and accountability.

Wiley (1994, p.41) suggests that there is now a general acceptance amongst OECD countries that quality is 'an essential ingredient in any reform agenda' and that efficiency and effectiveness are now the 'twin objectives' at the top of national health care agendas. Moreover, there is the argument elsewhere that, at a time of cost-containment in the light of increasing demands, it is even more important to focus on quality.

> In its simplest form the argument is that as increasing numbers of people make demands on static or diminishing resources, efforts must be made to ensure that the best possible care is made available to the greatest possible number of patients. This involves expunging waste from the system, using available resources as efficiently as possible, addressing issues of distribution and allocation of resources and, finally, ensuring that care delivered through the application of resources is effective in achieving appropriate outcomes (Ellis and Whittington 1993, pp.30-31).

Other concerns amongst OECD countries relate to customer satisfaction, or more specifically, the causes of dissatisfaction and the loss of people or physicians from the public system on the basis of concerns about quality (Kalisch et al, 1998).

GENERAL INTERNATIONAL
APPROACHES TO QUALITY

A number of specific themes can be identified in approaches to improving quality in health services or current thinking about quality from the work of Kalisch et al (1998), Boyce et al (1997) and Buchan (1998).

Central direction on defining and managing quality across health systems is common. National bodies with responsibility for developing national quality standards for health care have been established (Australia, Austria, Canada, France, Mexico, Britain and the USA) as have bodies to disseminate information on government-wide health care quality initiatives and goals (Germany, Australia, Austria and Belgium). Nation-wide performance standards and quality assurance programmes to encourage the development of high-quality health care delivery systems are in place in Spain, Sweden, Australia, Canada, France, Mexico, Belgium, Denmark, Austria and the US. In some countries this approach includes mandatory or voluntary accreditation programmes.

Financial incentives have been put in place to increase quality in France and Turkey. Quality has been tied into contracting in Italy. In Germany, contracted GPs and specialists are responsible for ensuring the quality, scope and economic efficiency of care. Quality is also being improved through competition. For instance, the separation of insurer from provider so that the insurer can specifically select providers offering a good range of services at an affordable price, as in Australia and Turkey. Or, patients being given the right to select and change their insurer, as in Germany and the Netherlands, or giving them the right to select their family physician, as in Turkey.

Accountability for quality and responsibility for monitoring quality and safety usually rests with professionals on a self-motivated basis. There is a shift from the professional accountability model to models of clinical governance and peer review. In Britain clinical governance puts a statutory responsibility on providers for the quality of care. More recently there has been a further shift towards external/objective quality validation.

In the monitoring and reviewing process, we see a shift from a focus on structure to one on process and more recently outcomes. The need to develop good information on the overall performance of the health care delivery systems and clinical information systems is being acknowledged. There is an increased emphasis on the use of quality indicators, partly because of improved data management systems, and partly due to a shift in emphasis from quality control/assurance to a focus on quality improvement. Lately, the emphasis has been on continuous quality improvement (CQI). There is also a move from the use of individual indicators on an ad-hoc basis to the development of whole sets of quality and outcome indicators. A pattern is emerging where there is a shift in quality management from a focus on acute hospital services to the evaluation of the performance of integrated healthcare systems. The need is seen to address inappropriate variations in clinical practice and services. Consumer empowerment and consumer participation in defining, managing and monitoring safety and quality of care are also coming to the fore.

A COMPARATIVE REVIEW OF APPROACHES ACROSS COUNTRIES

In the next sections, approaches to improving quality in health services in the following areas are discussed: national, centrally-driven approaches taken to improving quality across systems; external validation and accreditation; clinical audit; benchmarking; evidence-based practice; and health technology assessment.

NATIONAL, CENTRALLY-DRIVEN APPROACHES

The reforms launched for the National Health Service (NHS) in **Britain** in 1991, designed to improve quality through competition, had little impact (Klein, 1998). Further reforms in 1997 had a particular focus on quality improvement and were aimed at using central direction and control to make the NHS more quality conscious. The white paper, *A First Class Service:*

Quality in the new NHS (NHSE, 1998), outlines three key quality issues to be pursued through the reforms. The NHS should guarantee fair access and high quality to patients wherever they live. Issues of services falling short of patient expectations and recent publicised lapses in quality should be addressed. There should be a focus on tackling inequalities in terms of: variations in performance and practice, availability of new treatments, waiting times for operations, waiting times for test results and availability of screening.

The white paper outlines a ten-year programme of modernisation based around a number of initiatives and frameworks and the establishment of two new organisations.

To ensure fair access to effective, prompt, high-quality care wherever a patient receives treatment in the NHS, clear national standards for services will be developed, and consistent, evidence-based guidance will be issued in order to raise quality standards. In order to marry clinical judgement with clear national standards, there will be a particular emphasis on matching consistency in quality across the NHS with sensitivity to the needs of the individual patient and the local community. An annual national survey will seek the views of patients and users on their experience of health services.

National Service Frameworks will be developed for particular conditions and will address the whole system of care for that condition. They will be evidence-based and focus on how services can best be organised and on what standards should be met.

The NHS Performance Assessment Framework is intended to provide a more balanced view of NHS performance by focusing on six main areas: health improvement; fair access to services; effective delivery of appropriate care; efficiency; patient and carer experience; and health outcomes of NHS care. It is expected to have a central role in accountability and to underpin planning and management in the NHS.

It is also intended that clinical governance will provide the framework for assuring quality on clinical decisions. In addition, the newly formed National Institute for Clinical Excellence (NICE) will provide clear guidance for clinicians on which treatments work best. It will promote clinical and cost effectiveness through guidance and audit. It will also advise on best practice in the use of existing treatments and appraise new interventions and advise on their introduction along side existing options. In addition it will advise on clinical audit methodologies.

The Commission for Health Improvement (CHI) will have a statutory role in providing an independent guarantee that local systems to monitor, assure and improve clinical quality are in place. It will also have a role in supporting local organisations, and investigating problems and working with organisations to remedy such problems.

Leatherman and Sutherland (1998) suggest that the approach to quality management in Britain has evolved into a pyramid structure with three levels – strategic, operational and local. At the apex of the pyramid is the strategic, with the Department of Health NHS Executive providing the policy framework through a number of white papers which put quality at the top of the NHS agenda. Also at the strategic level are the institutions – NICE and CHI – and the national frameworks. Linking the strategic with the next level – the operational level – are performance indicators and performance contracts. At the base of the pyramid – the local level – quality is managed through peer review, clinical governance and quality monitoring approaches adopted by individual providers.

In **Canada** the national strategy for quality and effectiveness in health care attempts to achieve consensus across all levels on what constitutes quality and priority actions. Health Canada (1999) reports that there is co-ordinated research on policy, evaluation, the determinants of health and the validation of clinical indicators for identifying problem areas. Integrated information systems to provide meaningful data for providers and evaluators and to disseminate information are in place. Consensus is sought on strategies and mechanisms to implement quality management. Communication to distribute information on quality management developments and to develop Continuous Quality Improvement (CQI) networks is seen as important, as is improved evaluation of TQM existing initiatives and developing research on public and provider satisfaction. The development of practice guidelines is co-ordinated and studies of utilisation and appropriateness of services is undertaken as are outcome studies.

Health Canada (1999) also reports an increased emphasis there on quality of care and on developing mechanisms to improve and assess quality. Health Canada has a role in promoting partnership and coalitions towards a collaborative approach to developing a comprehensive strategy for the management of quality, aimed at CQI, enhancing responsiveness and effectiveness and involving everyone who is part of the health system.

In **Australia** a national Taskforce on Quality in Australian Health Care was established in 1995 following the findings of government funded research of a high prevalence of adverse events in hospitals. The taskforce identified the need to introduce a systematic approach to quality in health care. It placed the responsibility on organisers and managers of health care for creating and maintaining a system providing safe and quality care. Equally, it stressed the responsibility of practitioners for the standard of their own practice and shared responsibility for the system and the need for the involvement of all workers in improving safety and quality, along with consumers. It promoted evidence-based practice, consumer-focused services and consumer participation in quality management, with access for all providers to information systems about the quality of the care they provide. Consistent and regular monitoring and reporting of safety and quality of the system and component parts is necessary. Information on safety, quality and outcomes of care must be available to all those who want it and consumers must have ready access to effective complaint systems.

A National Expert Advisory Group on Safety and Quality was established to make practical suggestions to improve safety and quality in Australian hospitals and to direct and influence initiatives for acting on the recommendations of the taskforce.

External validation and accreditation
The central tenet of external validation is the provision of independent objective assessment and approval of the quality of care provided by health care organisations and approaches to quality management.

One approach to external validation currently gaining popularity is hospital accreditation. The accrediting body provides the framework for assessment and in purchaser/provider systems there are clear incentives to achieving accreditation. Several countries are looking at how hospital accreditation has developed in the **USA** and **Canada** with a view to developing similar systems. In the US, the Joint Commission on

Accreditation of Healthcare Organisations (JCAHO, 1999) is pushing for a national oversight system for healthcare organisations. In order to ensure that organisations 'do the right things and do them well', the JCAHO proposes the development of a standards-based evaluation framework, relating sound processes to good practice outcomes. It sees a need for appropriate measurement systems to be developed. Further, the capacity to evaluate all levels of the system needs to be developed and consensus is required on the best evaluation tools, with co-ordination required on evaluation activities.

Organisations accredited by the JCAHO receive triennial site visits, are involved in benchmarking and share information on good practice and exemplary performance. JCAHO is an advocate of Continuous Quality Improvement (CQI) and organisations accredited use performance measurement data to: provide continuous access to objective data in support of claims of quality; provide early warning of problems; verify the effectiveness of corrective actions; identify areas of excellence in the organisation; and compare performance with that of peer organisations using the same measures. The Canadian Council on Health Services Accreditation provides a similar programme of accreditation, using national standards developed for various types of services and organisations.

Also in the US, the Healthcare Financing Administration is the body responsible for the administration of the two federal health programmes – Medicare and Medicaid. It is responsible for implementing federal quality assurance standards for all of its health care providers. The approaches taken include: review and inspections by state inspection teams; peer review of the necessity, appropriateness and acceptability of services; and the 'health care quality improvement initiative', which emphasises the need for systematic assessment of care patterns and outcomes.

In **Australia**, the Australian Council on Health Care Standards (ACHS) is developing standards for the evaluation of patient care as the basis for voluntary accreditation of health care providers. Two programmes – EQUIP and CEP – were launched for quality improvement. The EQUIP programme (Evaluation of Quality Improvement Program) was developed by the ACHS to help organisations strive for excellence; organisations receive accreditation once specific standards have been met. The CEP

(Care Evaluation Program) is aimed at developing objective measures for the management and outcomes of patient care in acute health care organisations. Quality indicators are being developed in collaboration with medical colleges and associations.

In **New Zealand**, the Health Accreditation Programme for New Zealand (HAPNZ) is the national framework developed by Quality Health New Zealand. The programme is aimed at enabling health care organisations to improve their overall performance, develop strong leadership, enhance teamwork, develop effective clinical and management systems, improve their client focus, and enjoy a culture of continuous quality improvement (Quality Health New Zealand, 2001). They work with organisations through a process of self-assessment, an organisation-wide survey, quality action planning, accreditation, and the assessment of progress.

Safety and quality are promoted as primary objectives in current **French** health service reforms, which also emphasise the rights of patients and require organisations to assess patient satisfaction. A key element of the reforms is the introduction of accreditation and evaluation of professional and organisational practice. In particular, French hospitals are now required by law to set up accreditation systems, under guidance from a national agency for health service accreditation – ANAES (Segouin and Thayer, 1999).

Hospital accreditation is a new concept in **Britain** and the King's Fund Organisational Audit Unit is taking the lead in the development of hospital accreditation there. In Britain, the Audit Commission was established in 1990 with specific responsibility to carry out external audits of public services, including national health services. The work of the Audit Commission includes mandatory 'value for money' reviews of services, focusing on the effectiveness, efficiency and economy of services provided by health authorities and NHS trusts.

More recently, there has been growing interest in comparative analysis of accreditation frameworks and in countries learning from each other – a kind of peer review of accreditation frameworks, which would establish international credibility for accreditation and possibly result, in the longer-term, in the establishment of global criteria. Three specific projects along these lines are outlined by Heidemann (2000): the

ExPeRT Project funded by the EU, commenced in 1996; the 'Wellington Group' project, which commenced with an evaluation of the Health Accreditation Programme in New Zealand; and the ALPHA project commenced by the ISQua's accreditation subgroup.

Clinical Audit

The term clinical audit refers to a process through which professionals systematically review the care and treatment they provide to patients. Depending on the professionals involved, it may also be referred to as medical audit, therapy audit or nursing audit. A multidisciplinary approach may also be employed. It involves the examination of procedures, use of resources and outcomes of care, making changes wherever necessary. One of the aspirations in the development of clinical audit is that it should become a routine part of clinical practice. The clinical audit cycle begins with an evaluation of patient care against standards or professional guidelines. Recommendations are then made for changes in practice where improvements are required. A vital and often neglected part of the clinical audit cycle is referred to as 'closing the loop'. This involves a re-evaluation of care to ensure that recommendations have been implemented and have resulted in improvements. Further examination and recommended changes may be required if improvements have not been achieved.

Benchmarking

Benchmarking is a process that has been used a lot in industry and is becoming more common in healthcare. The European Foundation for Quality Management describes benchmarking as:

> The process of systematically comparing your own organisation structure, processes and performance against those of good practice organisations globally, with a view to achieving business excellence (EFQM, 1999).

The process is based around an organisation identifying role-model organisations with which it can make comparisons in order to identify performance gaps. Members of the EFQM use the business excellence model as the basis for comparisons. The EFQM reports that the use of the model in health care across Europe is 'emerging but fragmented'.

The approach to benchmarking in Britain involves three strands:

- *Standards benchmarking* – setting a standard for the organisation to achieve, for example the standards set out in the Patient's Charter in 1992.
- *Results benchmarking* – comparative analysis of achievements between similar organisations, for example comparisons of waiting times.
- *Process benchmarking* – the use of benchmarking to compare processes.

Evidence-based practice
The evidence-based approach is perhaps most developed in **Britain**. The central tenet in this approach is that treatments used should be shown to be effective and those that are not should be abandoned. It requires professionals to base their clinical judgements on sound research evidence, rather than relying solely on professional experience. In Britain centres such as the NHS Centre for Reviews and Dissemination (CRD) conduct research and systematic reviews to provide professionals and managers with the information required to make evidence-based decisions. In addition, there is an increased emphasis in professional education on how to critically review research and the appropriate application of findings to practice. The Cochrane Collaboration began as a Cochrane centre in Oxford in 1992 and since then has grown to become an international collaboration. Its original purpose was to disseminate the results of reviews of controlled trials on pregnancy and childbirth. Since then its role has expanded to include systematic reviews of all areas of healthcare.

In **Canada** the Health Services Research Fund supports research on improving evidence-based decision making in healthcare, treatment and prevention. In the **US**, the Agency for Healthcare Policy and Research funds evidence-based practice centres that link in with the development of clinical indicators for performance measurement.

Health Technology Assessment
Health Technology Assessment (HTA) is being carried out in several countries in the light of the burgeoning range of new technologies emerging in health care. The approach is aimed at providing an independent review of both new and existing technologies. For example, in **Australia** the National Health

Technology Advisory Council is responsible for the assessment of both emerging and existing technologies. In addition it is responsible for the development of guidelines for planning and delivery of specialised health services. Abel-Smith et al (1995) report a variety of approaches to HTA across EU countries. They report that approaches include the establishment of centres for the evaluation of health technologies, such as the National Commission for Hospital Planning in **Belgium**, or to development of assessment methodologies such as the Agence Nationale pour le developpement de l'Evaluation Medicale in **France**. Saltman and Figueras (1997) report that governments tend to play a major direct or indirect role in the development of health technology assessment, mainly to ensure independence of commercial influence and concern about some research undertaken by the pharmaceutical and medical equipment industries. Thus, the agencies that have been established in France, **Germany** and **Spain** (although established at regional level in Spain) are very closely linked to government. In other countries, the approach is decentralised, with research undertaken by universities but as part of a national framework of commissioned research. A third approach, identified by Saltman and Figueras, is for agencies responsible for paying for health care, including sickness funds and insurance agencies, to undertake the research. The general approach is to identify existing and emerging technologies and to evaluate them on the basis of existing evidence which is collected and analysed, or where appropriate, to conduct evaluative research. A key element of the approach is the dissemination of findings. Despite these developments, Abel-Smith et al (1995) suggest that HTA in Europe is largely an informal process and could be improved through better circulation of information produced through assessment activities and by clinicians having more timely access to findings, better resourcing and co-ordination of HTA activities. Saltman and Figueras (1997) suggest that much of clinical practice is still inadequately evaluated despite the considerable volume of activity being undertaken, largely because of the growth of health care technology and because the contexts within which technologies are used are also frequently changing.

While not wishing to be drawn on which structure is most effective, Saltman and Figueras (1997, p.198) identify several key tasks that should be undertaken in health technology assessment:

- a systematic identification of priorities based on national circumstances and a review of existing information
- reviews of existing evidence and basic research
- a means of ensuring that the results are collated in accessible form
- mechanisms for disseminating and implementing them (such as regulation, financial incentives and education).

WHAT ARE THE LESSONS FOR IRELAND?

A comparative review of approaches to quality improvement in various health systems shows that quality improvement is high on the agenda across countries. Approaches include national strategies, the development of national frameworks for performance standards and monitoring, the establishment of systems for external accreditation and validation, voluntary and conjoint working initiatives and a range of local approaches to CQI.

In Ireland, centrally driven approaches to developing quality have yet to be developed, a point emphasised in the 2001 strategy.

To date many quality initiatives have been undertaken although not necessarily as part of an overall co-ordinated plan. It is now time to embed quality more deliberately into the health system through comprehensive and co-ordinated national and local programmes (p. 19).

Pre-1994 quality management approaches were 'separate and individually driven' (Leahy 1998a, p. 152), and the development of a more co-ordinated approach will require considerable leadership at the national level. *Shaping a Healthier Future* (1994) emphasised the need to re-orientate health services towards consumer responsiveness. The strategy gave the Charter of Rights for Hospital Patients (first introduced in 1992) a central role in achieving this and stated that further charters will follow. Clinical audit, the measurement of patient satisfaction and the encouragement of health authorities to develop quality initiatives are also included in the measures identified towards improving quality. However, although launched in 1994, efforts in these areas are very much in their infancy and others have stalled. Building on this, the 2001 strategy aims to create a quality culture across all areas of the health system underpining all aspects of planning, management and the delivery of health services. The measures outlined to achieve this include:

- the development of a quality culture through an interdisciplinary approach, on-going education and commitment from healthcare institutions and professionals
- the establishment of a Health Information and Quality Authority as an independent statutory body with explicit responsibility to develop standards and to monitor services against those standards
- the development of national protocols for uniformly high quality care (p.11), for risk management and patient safety
- the development of standardised quality stems to support best patient care and safety, to facilitate regular evaluation and benchmarking of services and to provide a planned and systematic approach to quality assurance
- hospital accreditation
- the establishment of the Social Services Inspectorate on a statutory basis, with an extended remit to inspect residential care for people with disabilities and older people
- the development of risk management and evidence-based practice
- the development of a high-standard, well-integrated and reliable information system to provide the evidence for decision making and to provide feedback on the quality of care received and delivered
- a national patient satisfaction survey and complaints procedure.

Quality of service is also included in the objectives outlined by the Department of Health and Children in its 1998 strategy statement. The emphasis on quality is underpinned in national strategy documents such as the National Cancer Strategy and the Cardiovascular Strategy, where the aim is to provide safe, high quality services. These reports and the two recent health strategies (1994 and 2001) also emphasise the importance of evidence-based practice and the evaluation of the effectiveness of care and prevention, equity, accountability and audit. It should also be noted that there is a close relationship between concepts of quality and the concepts of performance measurement outlined in Chapter Seven.

The Irish Society for Quality in Healthcare was established in 1994. The society's aim is to 'improve the quality of healthcare nationally through partnership with all involved'. It is clear from the society's database of current quality initiatives that numerous quality initiatives and projects are underway around the country at local level. Through its multidisciplinary membership, the society seeks to share, promote and expand quality concepts throughout the Irish health system.

The society's President, Austin Leahy (1998a and 1998b), suggests that Ireland should move towards a national accreditation system, at least on a voluntary basis. In terms of quality assurance, he suggests that the way forward in Ireland is through two approaches. The first is the development of comparative audit. He reports that there are a number of regional audit projects being organised currently. He cites the Maryland QIP (Leahy, 1998b) as an example of how this could develop. The second approach which he puts forward is the development of continuous quality improvement (CQI). He suggests that this approach is less well developed than comparative audit in Ireland, mainly due to cultural obstructions and barriers between professionals, the lack of a multidisciplinary approach and inadequate allocation of resources for quality initiatives.

In our comparative review, several central drivers to developing quality management have been identified, such as the use of incentives and the introduction of clinical governance, that could be used to enhance the measures set out in the 2001 strategy. The emphasis in the strategy on patient satisfaction surveys, the development of CQI and hospital accreditation, and the establishment of the Health Information and Quality Authority, are consistent with current thinking on best practice in other countries. Evidence-based practice and health technology involvement are also key themes internationally. The challenge now will be to see this comprehensive range of measures implemented in a timely and co-ordinated way, to reach all levels and all parts of the health system. In addition, a number of departments and service areas have been successful in achieving ISO accreditation or the Q-Mark.

Although it received less attention in the 2001 *Health Strategy,* clinical audit was promoted in the 1994 *Health Strategy* as fundamental to the provision of quality health care, and it stated that 'all health professionals contributing to patient care fall within the scope of this process (p.25)'. The strategy also identified three key principles for the promotion of clinical audit and states that 'a programme of action to support and promote clinical audit will be drawn up through discussions with the various parties involved …'. Leahy (1998a) outlines four different types of audit and discusses a regional audit programme provided by the Royal College of Surgeons in Ireland. However, this programme is operated on a voluntary basis and the introduction of the Freedom of Information (FoI) legislation is known to have slowed down participation in the programme. Three clinical audit units have been established under the auspices of three health boards.

Within health boards, different approaches have been taken to addressing quality. This can include the development of a quality strategy and the promotion of a CQI approach across health service management activities. Benchmarking has yet to be established, but fifteen hospitals recently participated in a benchmarking study of patient satisfaction. Examples of the promotion of evidence-based practice are to be found in the national cancer and cardiovascular strategies.

This review suggests that the quality of health services has not received the same attention or level of promotion that it has in other countries and that efforts aimed explicitly at developing a quality culture are relatively recent in Ireland. However, the range of measures outlined in the 2001 strategy represent a significant commitment to the development of a quality agenda in Irish health services. The establishment of the National Healthcare Accreditation Board should provide an opportunity to refocus efforts on quality, but this applies only to the acute hospital sector and ways in which such approaches could be extended to other health services over the longer-term need to be considered. Other recent developments in health service management, such as the inclusion of performance indicators in service plans and the devolution of responsibility and accountability to health boards and managers, could also provide managers with the licence to develop innovative ways to continuously improve the quality of health services. The work done by the Irish Society for Quality in Healthcare, to compile an inventory of quality initiatives around the country, suggests that this sort of work is already underway in many centres but on an ad-hoc basis. This review suggests that managers could be further supported and guided in their efforts and that a sharing of experiences and lessons learned would also benefit managers and professionals. We would also suggest that some thought could be given to how other existing efforts, such as the regional clinical audit programmes, could be adapted and applied in other regions and across professional areas.

Chapter 9
The Voluntary Sector
in the Health Services

INTRODUCTION

In the last decade or so, considerable discussion has taken place on the role of the Irish voluntary sector in the health services and elsewhere. Significant publications, including a green paper (Department of Social Welfare, 1997) and white paper (Department of Social, Community and Family Affairs, 2000) *Supporting Voluntary Activity* have appeared. Academic writing in this area has developed considerably and several Irish universities have set up specific research groups devoted to voluntary sector research.

How is the voluntary sector viewed elsewhere? What are the issues it faces in the health services elsewhere? What are its links with the state? This chapter will consider these issues. More specifically, it will consider definitional and measurement issues relative to the voluntary sector. It will look at the respective roles of the voluntary sector and of the state in the health services and at issues of cooperation between the state and voluntary organisations. It will seek to take account of trends in the voluntary sector elsewhere and of significant themes in the comparative literature on this topic.

WHAT IS THE ISSUE IN IRELAND AND WHY IS IT IMPORTANT?

There is no doubting the importance of the voluntary sector in the Irish health services. That sector, the *Health Strategy* stated in 1994, 'plays an integral role in the provision of health and personal social services in Ireland which is perhaps unparalleled in any other country' (p.33). The Commission on Health Funding in 1989 highlighted the 'immensely important' role of voluntary organisations and referred to their community spirit, humanitarianism and closeness to the client group (para. 17.32).

In acute hospital and intellectual disability services and in care of the elderly and child care, voluntary agencies in Ireland make an enormous contribution to the health services. The white paper *Supporting Voluntary Activity* (Department of Social, Community and Family Affairs, 2000) reported that the health boards disbursed around £390 million to community/voluntary agencies in 1999 (excluding acute hospitals). *Health Statistics* in 1999 indicated that spending on the services of public voluntary hospitals amounted to over £518 million in 1996. In 1995, according to *Enhancing the Partnership* (Department of Health and Children, 1997), direct funded mental handicap agencies — that is, those agencies which at that time were funded directly by the Department of Health and Children — received funds of £126 million, out of a total estimated health expenditure on services to persons with a mental handicap or intellectual disability of over £250 million (p.17).   According to Health Statistics in 1999, public voluntary hospitals account for around 45 per cent of all acute hospital beds in Ireland and 42 per cent of all admissions.

If this picture of the voluntary sector appears very positive, discussion of the voluntary sector also raises important issues and tensions. For example, statistics on the sector are limited in Ireland (and elsewhere). Voluntary agencies have also been subject to considerable questioning and criticism, particularly in relation to accountability. Questions have been raised about the appropriate relationship between the voluntary sector and the state and about how the voluntary sector is likely to develop, or should develop, in the future.

In Ireland, major changes have taken place in how the voluntary sector is constituted. Jaffro (1996) examined the historical development of the voluntary sector in Ireland. She referred to the influence of religious and self-help organisations in the nineteenth and twentieth centuries and to a more recent 'new wave' of community-based organisations, sometimes supported by EU funding. The Catholic Church made an enormous contribution to the voluntary sector in the past. The decline in religious vocations and the reorienting of Catholic priorities towards the Third World have reduced that contribution and are likely to continue to do so in the years ahead.

There are serious definitional issues and debates in relation to the voluntary sector. Some question for example whether public voluntary hospitals are voluntary agencies in any meaningful sense and are rather 'reluctant and awkward building blocks of an integrated and more centrally controlled health system' (O'Ferrall, 2000, p. 272). This chapter will seek to illuminate some of these issues through a comparative examination of the voluntary sector.

Issues relating to the voluntary sector include both practical and policy-oriented questions. What is the size of the voluntary sector in Ireland and specifically in the health services? How is the sector likely to develop in the future and how should it develop in the future? What is its appropriate relationship with the state? How does the voluntary sector in Ireland compare with that in other countries?

These questions will be examined in a comparative framework in this chapter

INTERNATIONAL PERSPECTIVES ON THE VOLUNTARY SECTOR

As noted at the outset, the Irish 1994 *Health Strategy* described the role of the voluntary sector in Ireland as unparalleled. While the voluntary sector is certainly a very significant reality in Ireland, it is difficult to compare it in a precise way to the voluntary sector in other countries because comparative international data is very scarce in this area. Discussion of the voluntary sector in Ireland has been hampered by this lack of data and by the difficulty of international comparison.

In the Johns Hopkins *Non-profit Sector Series*, Salamon and Anheier (1997) have done important work in attempting to arrive at a common international definition and classification of voluntary bodies. They define what they call 'non-profit organisations' as organisations that are: organised, that is, institutionalised to some extent, or formally constituted; private, that is, institutionally separate from government; non-profit-distributing; self-governing; and voluntary to some significant degree (pp.33-34).

They note that the 'private' characteristic does not exclude the possibility of significant government funding or prevent government officials from sitting on their boards: 'The key here is that non-profit organisations must be fundamentally private institutions in basic structure' (p.33).

The 'voluntary' characteristic does not mean either that most of the income of an organisation must come from voluntary contributions, or that most of its staff must be volunteers. The definitional requirement here is that there be 'some meaningful degree of voluntary participation either in the actual conduct of the agency's activities, or in the management of its affairs. The presence of some voluntary input, even if only a voluntary board of directors, suffices to qualify an organisation as in some sense voluntary' (p.34).

Although some in Ireland question the classification of the voluntary hospitals, it is clear that the larger, publicly-funded voluntary agencies in Ireland – for example, the public voluntary hospitals and the large mental handicap agencies – qualify as voluntary organisations under the Salamon/Anheier definition and indeed must be included in the Irish voluntary sector if it is to be compared to the voluntary sector elsewhere on the basis of the Johns Hopkins (Salamon/Anheier) classification.

Applying their definition in detail to seven different countries – the US, UK, France, Germany, Italy, Hungary and Japan, but not Ireland – Salamon and Anheier (1996) found that the non-profit sector accounted for one out of every twenty jobs and one out of every eight service jobs, and the operating expenditure of non-profit organisations accounted for 4.5 per cent of GDP in those seven countries. The US had the largest non-profit sector in both absolute and relative terms, with 6.9 per cent of total employment. In France, Germany and the UK, the non-profit sector accounted for 3-4 per cent of all jobs and 9-10 per cent of all employment in the service sector. They also found that in Japan and the UK, the dominant field of non-profit activity is education. In Germany and the US it is health. In France and Italy it is social services. In Hungary it is culture and recreation. And in the developing countries, it is development, broadly defined (pp.xiii-xix).

APPLYING AN INTERNATIONAL
FRAMEWORK TO IRELAND

Applying the international framework established by the Johns Hopkins International study on the non-profit sector, Donoghue et al (1999) attempted to measure the size of the voluntary sector in Ireland. In the absence of nationally gathered data on that sector, they acknowledged that their estimates must be seen as approximate. Making due allowance for such approximation, it is nevertheless interesting to report their findings.

They estimated that the 1995 income of the voluntary sector (non-health and health, including the public voluntary hospitals and the large mental handicap agencies) amounted to £3.24 billion, 8.2 per cent GDP or 9.3 per cent GNP. If volunteering is taken into account, the figures rise to 9.45 per cent GNP and 8.6 per cent GDP. Some £2.4 billion, almost three quarters of the income of £3.24 billion, came from the state. Of this figure of £2.4 billion, around 29 per cent went to the health sector

The total income of voluntary organisations in the health sector amounted to almost £783 million with close to 90 per cent of this figure coming from public sources.

In relation to staffing, Donoghue et al (1999) report, there were over 125,000 people in paid employment in the non-profit sector, including nearly 33,000 people in the health sector. The overall figure of 125,000 constituted 12 per cent of the non-agricultural workforce; however, if volunteering is taken into account, the figure rose to 15 per cent of that workforce.

In relation to the voluntary and community sector – which they defined as including voluntary and community organisations in a wide range of categories but excluding hospitals, hospices, primary, secondary and tertiary educational institutions – Donoghue et al found that this sector accounted for over 6 per cent of the non-agricultural labour force.

Donoghue et al compared Ireland to other countries analysed under the Johns Hopkins framework. They found that Ireland was second only to the Netherlands in terms of the number of people working in the non-profit sector (as a percentage of the non-agricultural labour force). On the other hand, the numbers of volunteers in Ireland was lower than the EU average.

The expenditure of the non-profit sector in Ireland was also well above the EU average (9.5 per cent GDP as against 8.7 per cent GDP)

Of all the countries surveyed, Ireland was the most dependent on public sector support for the non-profit sector. According to a publication by Salamon, Anheier and Associates (1998), this support accounted for 74.5 per cent of the cash revenue of the non-profit sector in Ireland (compared to an EU average of 54.8 per cent)

The Johns Hopkins framework has made a significant contribution to the study of the voluntary or non-profit sector around the world and has clearly helped considerably in mapping the sector in Ireland.

The next section will consider some key aspects of the relationship between the state and the voluntary sector. An area dealt with rather briefly by the Johns Hopkins publications is that of the philosophical justification for the voluntary sector – a topic that will be considered in the final section of this chapter.

THEMES IN STATUTORY-VOLUNTARY LINKS

Funding and contracting in Ireland
Discussion of the state and the voluntary sector frequently focuses on the issue of funding. However, the white paper of 2000 usefully emphasised that the issues involved go well beyond funding alone: 'We have moved beyond the attitude that statutory agencies fund voluntary organisations merely for utilitarian reasons, i.e. to provide services that the state cannot or will not deliver directly because of resource constraints...' (p.iii).

In its analysis of funding, the white paper distinguished between non-governmental organisations (such as a voluntary hospital) that provide services by and on behalf of a statutory agency, and community and voluntary organisations that provide other services and undertake developmental activities to meet social need, without being delivery agencies on behalf of a statutory agency. The focus of the white paper is more on the second type of body – that is on the smaller community and voluntary bodies and on funding for such bodies.

In her study of funding in the Irish voluntary sector, Hayes (1999) concludes that statutory funding now constitutes a significant source of revenue for the Irish voluntary sector, in keeping with patterns in the UK and the US. She adds: 'However, it is not available to all organisations and even those which have access to it can often face challenges in complying with the requirements of the relevant statutory authority' (p.4).

Drawing on the research of Faughnan and Kelleher (1993), Donoghue (1999), Wall (1997) and others, Hayes lists some of these challenges: varied sources of funding, complicated methods of accountability, ad hoc and uncertain arrangements and great variations in the levels of state funding to different voluntary organisations.

Faughnan and Kelleher (1993) point to two possible definitions of contracting: (a) a narrow definition in which there is common agreement on the nature of the service, targets, resources and criteria for monitoring; and (b) a wider concept in which there is provision for consultation and negotiation with the voluntary sector on the scope and implementation of a service as well as on the broader policy and administrative framework.

Some of those interviewed by Faughnan and Kelleher felt that contracting arrangements did not fit well with a campaigning, advocacy and policy development role on the part of the voluntary organisation. It certainly seems possible in principle that a vigorous campaigning stance by a voluntary organisation might from time to time provoke the wrath of a statutory organisation on which it was dependent for the provision of its contract.

O'Sullivan (1998) set out some recent developments in Ireland in the development of contracting and service agreements, including the negotiation in 1997 of the *Enhancing the Partnership* (Department of Health and Children, 1997) agreement between the state and the large voluntary organisations providing services in the mental handicap/intellectual disability sphere. This agreement provided for the funding of such organisations by the regional health boards rather than by the state; for the establishment of regional decision-making and consultative committees; for the development of service agreements between the health board and voluntary organisations; and (an aspect of particular importance for the voluntary side) for independent arbitration in the case of disputes.

Some legislative developments in Ireland have important implications for statutory-voluntary relationships. Thus the Health (No. 3) (Amendment) Act, 1996 – generally described as the accountability legislation – provides specific statutory recognition of the requirement for cooperation of the health board with the community and voluntary sector. The Health (ERHA) Act, 1999 provides that all funding of non-statutory agencies will be in the context of written service agreements which provide for annual renewal and review of funding. These agreements will cover a period of between three and five years, will set out the principles by which both parties agree to abide and will set out standards relating to efficiency, effectiveness and quality of service.

Funding and contracting in other countries

Funding and contracting issues are important in many countries. Salamon and Anheier (1997) note that in France the growing importance of the French non-profit sector is linked to the policy of decentralisation introduced by the Socialist government in the 1980s. Public financing, they note, accounts for over 50 per cent of the resources of important health and welfare associations. They suggest that the French government has used independent non-profit or 'social economy' organisations as vehicles to administer welfare and employment programmes. As Lebaube (1999) makes clear, the focus of French debate has been more on whether cooperative organisations can continue to preserve an identity which is distinct from that of conventional private companies or dissolve into capitalism. This is a quite different debate to the classic statutory-voluntary concerns of the Irish model.

The concerns about contracting listed by the voluntary sector in Ireland have also been articulated elsewhere. Thus, a 1990 UK Home Office document (Home Office, Great Britain, 1990), reported a strong mistrust among voluntary organisations towards contract funding; such organisations felt that contracting would limit their independence. Nevertheless, the voluntary organisations contacted for the Home Office report were in favour of 'clearer, more rational, more comprehensive and more accessible' grant application procedures (p.49). Johnson (1987), who was critical of the voluntary sector's 'uneven and incomplete coverage' (p. 122), argues that public funding 'carries a price': it entails a loss of independence and expectations of conformity (p. 121). However, he acknowledged that national experiences differ, with Dutch voluntary agencies (for example) retaining a lot of autonomy in spite of heavy reliance on state funding. Whelan (1997) offered a pessimistic perspective on British trends: 'Most of what we now call the voluntary sector isn't. The majority of charities … are effectively sub-contractors to the state welfare system… Voluntary work becomes defined as that which the government will pay for' (p.11).

On the basis of the experiences which they report in a wide range of countries, Salamon and Anheier (1996) state that

... the crucial issue is how to fashion cooperation with the State in a way that protects the non-profit sector from surrendering its basic autonomy and allows it to function as true partner rather than agent (p. 121).

They identify three important models of cooperation: (a) the German corporatist model in which there is obligatory consultation in advance of all major social legislation; (b) the US interest group model, in which opportunities are provided to non-profit organisations to influence legislation and budgets in an ad hoc way; (c) the British scrutiny approach, in which government agencies that fund voluntary organisations are required (in dialogue with the voluntary organisations) to clarify more precisely than in the past the objectives of services for which funding is required.

Kendall and Knapp (1996) sound a note of caution however about such a broad brush framework: 'such generalisations about the relationship between the sectors across all industries and contexts obviously should be treated with caution' (p. 253).

In the Irish context, close cooperation between the voluntary sector and the state is manifest in a number of ways. For example, the voluntary and community sector have been involved since the 1990s in the Irish partnership arrangements between the state, the employers, the unions and other key interest groups. Agencies can also influence policy and the annual budget in an ad hoc way.

Salamon and Anheier argue that to move towards partnership, the voluntary sector needs to develop its own funding, with the level of income coming from its own sources at a possible minimum of 10 per cent (though only in a few of the countries which they surveyed did voluntary organisations have such a level of self-generated funding). They call for other reforms such as liberalisation of tax incentives, the need for greater transparency by the non-profits and the need for more professionalisation in areas such as staff training and pay scales.

VARYING VIEWS ON THE RATIONALE FOR THE VOLUNTARY SECTOR

While issues of contracting and funding arrangements are very important, they are less fundamental than those relating to the rationale or justification for the voluntary sector. That sector has been subject to significant criticism or questioning in Ireland.

May public voluntary hospitals be considered as voluntary in any meaningful sense? Why should privately owned hospitals receive state funding if they are not to be totally subject to the control of the state authorities? If it is ultimately the state's responsibility to fund and provide social services, why should it attempt to offload this responsibility to voluntary organisations?

O'Sullivan (1999-2000) raises some of these questions. He maintains that fundamental tensions and contradictions within this sector need to be explored before pursuing ambitious agendas for these agencies in both the delivery and formulation of welfare in Ireland (p. 55). He argues for example that 'the control of significant elements of the infrastructure of the Irish welfare state by a relatively small number of voluntary/non-profit agencies severely limits the capacity of the state to ... meet welfare needs'. He also refers to a need for debate on 'the lack of accountability of these agencies to their funders or their clients' (pp. 61 and 63).

Discussion of the voluntary sector in Ireland has also been influenced by the Irish debate about subsidiarity – the principle that the state should not take over tasks which the individual, the family, the local association (or the voluntary organisation) can competently carry out themselves. Since the 1951 Mother and Child controversy (the failure of a government scheme, opposed by the Catholic bishops and the medical profession, to extend eligibility for maternity and infant services: see Whyte, 1980 and Barrington, 1987), subsidiarity has tended to be seen in Ireland as a conservative Catholic concept putting a brake on a necessary expansion of state services. Fanning (1999) refers to the Church's 'active resistance' up to the sixties to extending the role of the state in the provision of health and personal social services (p. 57). In so far as subsidiarity is an important philosophical justification for the voluntary sector, that sector has perhaps suffered, at least in academic debate, from its association with subsidiarity. Thus Peillon (1982) has criticised in trenchant terms the links between the Church and the voluntary sector: 'In defending the family unit and the independence of voluntary organisations, the Church was seeking to consolidate its own authority and influence. By means of voluntary associations, the Church can dominate such spheres of activity as health and social services' (p. 95).

An equally vigorous critique of the state, or at least of an overweening role for the state, may be found in some literature sympathetic to voluntary effort, for example, in the writings of Catholic philosophers such as Maritain (Evans and Ward, 1956), who referred to the risk of having 'too many functions of social life controlled by the State from above'. He argued that the state is:

> ... only that part of the body politic especially concerned with the maintenance of law, the promotion of the common welfare and public order, and the administration of public affairs. The state is a part which specialises in the interests of the whole ... (However) The state has been made an absolute, placed on top of the body politic rather than serving it (pp. 95 and 100).

More recently, an official Catholic document, *Centesimus Annus*, re-stated the Church's support for basic principles of solidarity and subsidiarity and referred to 'excesses and abuses ... (which) have provoked very harsh criticisms of the Welfare State'. The document made a strong case, at least by implication, for the contribution of voluntary organisations:

> Certain kinds of demands often call for a response which is not simply material but which is capable of perceiving the deeper human need. One thinks of the condition of refugees, immigrants, the elderly, the sick, and all those in circumstances which call for assistance, such as drug users: all those people can be helped effectively only by those who offer them genuine fraternal support, in addition to the necessary care (John Paul II, 1991, par. 48).

In a wide-ranging Irish review of comparative literature, O'Ferrall (2000) makes a case for 'a democratic theory of active citizenship in a pluralist society' (p.265) as a justification for voluntary effort and points to the fact that the term active citizenship was used in the 1997 green paper on the voluntary sector (Department of Social Welfare, 1997). He draws on the writings of Tocqueville and Mill as well as of more recent theorists and argues that 'the modern civic republican tradition provides a theoretical basis for a developed form of participatory democracy: civic republicans emphasise the intrinsic value of political participation for the participants themselves' (p. 101). O'Ferrall stresses the importance of the voluntary sector while questioning some traditional justifications for the sector. He criticises not the voluntary sector per se but what he sees as a (no longer relevant) religious-based justification for the sector (that is, subsidiarity).

He argues that the religious concept of subsidiarity is no longer of great value in a much more secular society: 'The religious justification, based on subsidiarity, while valuable and important, is insufficient to provide legitimacy in an increasingly secular society seeking to develop a public policy on the appropriate relationships between the state and voluntary organisations' (p. 79).

The view that subsidiarity is a religious or specifically Catholic concept is open to question. While it was strongly advocated by the Catholic Church in the twentieth century and explicitly from the 1930s, subsidiarity is neither specifically religious nor a concept of recent origin. Its theoretical origins have been traced to concepts of freedom and virtue in Plato and Aristotle (Finnis, 1980 and Hochshild, 2000). Hochshild argues that 'though it has been explicitly formulated only recently, the principle of subsidiarity is not ... a new principle'. Referring to the work of an important Protestant political theorist Johannes Althusius (1557-1638), Hochschild states that 'the general structure of Althusius's *Politica*, moving from the primary, most local and natural association – the family – up through different, progressively less local and less natural associations, parallels the structure of the beginning of Aristotle's *Politics*'.

The implication of this argument is that subsidiarity or allied concepts have provided over a long period a critique of the claims of a dominant state and at least an implicit justification of the role of the voluntary sector.

Clearly, examination of the comparative literature cannot dispel controversy about the voluntary sector and the state, since philosophical differences transcend national boundaries. It does however indicate that perspectives about the voluntary sector are greatly influenced by ideas about the role of the state.

Thus Pinker (1992) has provided a useful review of changing attitudes to the state in the British context. Although Beveridge (often seen as the father of the British welfare state) was convinced of the value of a flourishing voluntary sector, Pinker maintains that in the 1960s, the subject of social administration was bound by the restraints of a largely collectivist set of assumptions: 'It was taken for granted that the state had a dominant role to play as both funder and provider of social services' (p.273). In similar vein, Wilding (1992) argues that most students of social policy before the 1980s tended to be preoccupied with state welfare. A more critical view of the state was influenced by the collapse of Communism in the USSR and by the impact of the Thatcher years in Britain. According to Pinker, 'confidence in Marxism and classical political economy – the two great normative paradigms inherited from the eighteenth and nineteenth centuries – has been undermined' (by the events of the 1980s) (p. 273).

Johnson (1987) distinguishes between residual and institutional models of welfare. Those who favour the institutional model have a largely collectivist set of assumptions while the residual model is one in which the state plays a residual role. According to Pinker, this role 'is entirely compatible with a form of welfare pluralism in which the private and voluntary sectors have become the main funders and providers of social services' (1992, p. 278).

Johnson (1987) defines welfare pluralism as 'a reduction or reversal of the state's dominance in welfare provision and an increase in the role of the informal, voluntary and commercial sectors' (p. 54).

Pinker (1992) develops the definition by distinguishing between two forms of pluralism: 'There is one form of pluralism in which the range and variety of service provision is increased while the statutory authorities, both central and local, continue as the main source of funding. In another form, a new plurality of service providers is developed as an alternative to statutory funding, with the ultimate goal of privatising as much of the system as possible' (p. 278). Pinker's first category is clearly a more institutional form of pluralism and his second category a more residual form.

The residual-institutional debate in Britain in the past has tended to focus on the respective merits of the state and the market. In Ireland, since the debates of the 1950s, the debate has been less polarised, at least in relation to state/market categories. Proponents of the voluntary sector – whether they favour subsidiarity or alternative conceptions such as O'Ferrall's 'active citizenship' – have generally accepted that the state has an important role while subsidiarity has also made something of a comeback, principally through its espousal by the European Union.

Internationally, ideological differences on the role of the state have lessened in some respects with the fall of Communism in the USSR. Currin (1992), commenting on former totalitarian regimes in Eastern Europe and South Africa, emphasised the important role played by voluntary organisations in civil society and their contribution to democracy and development. Wilding (1992) refers to a general, though critical, acceptance of welfare pluralism in Britain in the 1980s – reflected for example in the new attention devoted in the academic world to the voluntary sector. The corollary of the re-examination of the role of the state has been a renewed interest in the role and possibilities of the voluntary sector.

WHAT ARE THE LESSONS FOR IRELAND?

Discussion of the voluntary sector in Ireland has sometimes appeared to operate on the assumption that that sector has a far greater importance in Ireland than in other countries. However, examination of the comparative literature indicates that it also is a very significant reality in many other countries.

Definitional and data problems have often been highlighted in Ireland but clearly important work has been done in this area by (for example) the international Johns Hopkins project which has developed both an international classification system and useful statistics. It is of interest to note that the white paper in 2000 indicated that the Irish government would be sponsoring further research on the size and extent of the voluntary sector in Ireland.

There is a need for clarity on the rationale for the voluntary sector. Terminology differs but clearly recent trends, such as the re-emergence of the concept of subsidiarity or the growth of 'welfare pluralism', point to a growing acceptance of the importance of the voluntary sector (where perhaps such acceptance was grudging in the past). As Pinker (1992) has argued in the British context, people thirty years ago were 'either collectivists or individualists, subscribing either to the idea of a predominantly statutory, institutional and unitary welfare state or to the alternative notion of residual welfare, in which the state merely provides a safety net for a small minority of citizens. Since then the quality of the debate has changed out of all recognition, and we are more inclined to consider policy options on their merits and without bias'.

As the 2000 white paper made clear (Department of Social, Community and Family Affairs, 2000), links between the statutory and voluntary sectors need to be well thought out, particularly in relation to funding approaches. Nevertheless, (as this document also suggested) discussion of the voluntary sector should not be limited to the question of funding appropriate bureaucratic mechanisms for statutory-voluntary coordination.

As the white paper put it, 'the government regards statutory support of the community and voluntary sector as having an importance to the well-being of our society that goes beyond 'purchase' of services by this or that statutory agency. The government's vision of society is one which encourages people and communities to look after their own needs – very often in partnership with statutory agencies – but without depending on the state to meet all needs' (pp. (iii) and 4).

Chapter 10
Conclusions

The 2001 *Health Strategy* has set out a direction for the Irish health services for the coming years, based on analysis of Irish issues and of experience elsewhere. Our hope is that this book will contribute in a modest way to the national discussion set in motion by the strategy. Like the strategy, though in a necessarily less prescriptive way, this book has considered current health issues in Ireland in a comparative context; and has also sought to look at possible learning for Ireland from experience elsewhere.

Comparative reflection points up strengths as well as shortcomings in one's own system and thus guards against the dangers both of complacency and of excessive self-criticism. If this book has pointed to some deficiencies or reform needs in the Irish health care system, it also acknowledges (as did the OECD report in 1997) the many strengths of the system and of those who work in the system.

The book began by setting out some general points about comparison – for example, Chapter 3 highlighted the importance of adequate frameworks for comparison. We referred in that chapter to some frameworks for comparison in the literature. Our approach in this book has been to develop comparisons between Ireland and other OECD countries on the basis of key themes such as health gain and service planning.

Any comparative study in health care must include some reflection about the goals of health care systems. As we noted in Chapter 1, *The World Health Report 2000* suggested that health care systems have three overall goals: health improvement; responsiveness to the expectations of the population; and fairness of financial contribution. It also maintained that systems have four vital functions: service provision, resource generation, financing and stewardship. The different chapters of this book have examined specific issues in the Irish health care system which are closely related to these goals and functions: for example, health gain (health improvement), quality

130

(responsiveness to the expectations of the population) and the public-private mix and performance measurement (stewardship).

Our comparative review has highlighted specific health care themes which we discuss in this concluding chapter.

STRUCTURAL REFORM

Comparative examination of the recent health care experience of many OECD countries reveals the variety and extent of structural reform in those countries and points to the need for regular review and analysis of the appropriateness of health care structures. We referred in Chapter 2 to some of the structural reforms undertaken in OECD countries in recent decades – including the separation of purchaser and provider functions (for example, New Zealand, Britain and Sweden), the establishment of new quality structures (Britain post-1997), decentralisation of structures or the establishment of new regional structures (Canada and France) or the development of new experimental care networks (France).

As indicated in Chapter 2, service integration is an important objective of structural reform in many countries. The establishment of new regional agencies in France and Canada and the substitution of broader-based primary care trusts for GP fund-holders in Britain were all intended to foster improved service integration.

A possible lesson from comparative analysis of structural reform is that there may sometimes be a case for piloting structural change or reform in one region, rather than simply introducing such change everywhere at the same time. The experimental care networks in France are an interesting example of small-scale pilots from which, it is hoped, the whole system can learn (though by definition at a slow pace). On the other hand, major purchaser-provider reforms with very ambitious objectives were introduced in Britain and Sweden in the 1990s but, as we have noted, these reforms had to be re-visited before the end of the decade. It should be added, however, that these reforms were studied with great interest elsewhere.

Chapter 2 drew attention to a widespread international interest in the Human Resource Management (HRM) area in the health services. As noted in that chapter, the HRM literature in other countries identified the importance of devolved responsibility for HRM. Another theme in the literature is that the success of structures and of structural reform depends fundamentally on the capacity of health services personnel. The literature therefore stresses the need for the capacity-building of such personnel. The 2001 *Health Strategy* in Ireland also highlighted as a key framework for change the development of human resources in the Irish health services.

There are close links between structural reforms and reform in management approaches and priorities. In Ireland, the need to reform structures to address the perceived confusion between policy and executive functions was recognised in the 1994 *Health Strategy* which set out a structure for the Department of Health to devolve its executive functions to health boards, and thus, to refocus its efforts on the development of national policy and system oversight. The establishment of the ERHA further supported devolution from the centre by shifting responsibility for the public voluntary hospitals from the Department of Health and Children to the ERHA. The planned establishment of the Health Boards Executive (HeBE) in March 2002 will also enable the department to further devolve functions that are not consistent with its emerging role.

The structural reforms proposed in the 1994 strategy were that boards should have more autonomy to perform their functions in an effective and efficient way, but within an explicit accountability framework. Such reforms are further reinforced in legislation, which sought to enhance accountability between the department and health boards, to clarify the responsibilities of health board chief executive officers and to require health boards to produce an annual service plan. There is also increasing emphasis on accountability between health boards and providers, with boards required to put more structured arrangements in place to measure their own performance and the performance of service provider agencies.

Finally, comparative study of structural reform in OECD countries in the 1990s suggests that such reform, however well designed, is not a panacea for health care problems. Such reform cannot act as a substitute for a strong ethical commitment to patient care on the part of health care professionals; or compensate for problems in the motivation of health care personnel or for shortages of key professionals. Nor can we be certain about the likely impact of such reform.

As the *World Health Report 2000* puts it:

Many questions about health system performance have no clear or simple answers – because outcomes are hard to measure and it is hard to disentangle the health system's contribution from other factors (WHO, 2000, p. xi).

The relationship, in other words, between health systems and health outcomes is complex and the impact of structural reform on the health of the citizen in Ireland or elsewhere is indirect rather than direct. Structural reform may be associated however with an improvement in quality – for example, the European Observatory on Health Care Systems (1999) suggested that GP fundholders in Britain succeeded in bringing about some improvements in the quality of services, albeit on a small scale (p. 108).

A *more pro-active approach to management*

A second theme to emerge from our analysis of reform in Ireland and elsewhere is a growing emphasis on enhancing the effectiveness of management, and taking a more proactive approach to planning. The review of service planning indicates some ways in which the roles of the various elements of a health system can be differentiated to bring greater clarity to the planning process and to improve the responsiveness of services to local needs. The roles of central and national agencies in the provision of direction on national health priorities and in monitoring progress against key objectives, are clearly very different to those at regional and local level, where the concern is primarily to ensure that services are responsive to local needs. However roles are complementary, and planning to meet both national and local needs involves a balanced mix of top-down and bottom-up analysis and decision making. We would also suggest that a greater emphasis on results, over and above inputs and processes, and greater flexibility in funding arrangements between the centre and regions (for example, a shift to multi-annual budgeting) would free up health resources to be redirected on health service priorities. However, where this has been pursued in other countries it has been within a clear, established accountability and reporting framework. Current thinking is that a focus on results, rather than on compliance with prescriptive practices, allows managers to fulfil their management role and supports creative thinking and innovative approaches to achieving results. Nonetheless, information on how results have been achieved is also important for learning and to support thinking in the development of future initiatives.

The development of performance measurement is a key element in health service reforms across countries and, as suggested from the comparative review presented in this book, Ireland can learn from the experiences of performance measurement in other countries. The work done to date across countries reflects an increasing emphasis on good governance, on demonstrating to tax payers that their investment in health services has been managed to achieve optimum returns and providing good information to support effective decision making. Economy, efficiency and effectiveness are key themes, but the review of performance measures across a sample of health systems also emphasises the importance of measures of quality, the perceptions of patients and carers, equity and of longer-term health outcomes.

The development of evaluation capacity is also an important aspect of the most recent reforms in Ireland and is the focus of a forthcoming Committee for Public Management Research discussion paper (Butler, 2002). Unlike performance measurement, where the emphasis is on developing and monitoring indicators of performance, evaluation is concerned with in-depth analysis of the performance of a particular policy, programme or project. However, evaluation and performance measurement are complementary and can be seen as two separate approaches to producing complementary data to support management decisions. Evaluation can help to understand some of the issues raised, and can indicate what is contributing to apparently poor or outstanding performance. Performance indicators can provide a broad assessment of performance across the range of areas of health service provision or elements of a service, and thus identify areas of concern and priorities for evaluation.

In Ireland, there is evidence of an increasing interest in evaluation in health services. Examples are to be found of analysis to inform the development of particular strategies, to monitor progress during the implementation of an initiative, to inform corrective action and to assess the effectiveness of particular projects or programmes. International thinking on evaluation stresses three key points. First, evaluation has a vital role to play in accountability, effective management, decision making and organisational learning. Second, it is no longer seen as solely an external activity conducted by specialist evaluators, but as a key element of effective project management and an activity that feeds into decision making throughout the life of a project, initiative or programme. Third, a participative approach is best and evaluation should be focused, at the design stage, on the data needs of those who will ultimately use the findings as the basis for decision making.

The rise of performance measurement and evaluation are part of an increased emphasis on evidence-based management and service review; on demonstrating that something works (or does not) rather than taking this for granted; and on a more rational approach to planning, needs assessment and prioritising. It also places management information centre stage in reforms.

The emphasis in current approaches to quality management, as outlined in Chapter 8, is on stitching quality into service design and on continuous assessment of an organisation's efforts to monitor and improve quality. Once again, the provision of central direction is a key aspect of efforts in many countries, along with the development of incentives to demonstrate improved quality and the development of quality indicators. There is also an emphasis on empowering consumers and enabling them to participate in the design and monitoring of services. These approaches are complemented with developments in the areas of external accreditation, clinical audit, benchmarking, evidence-based practice and health technology assessment.

By comparison, formal efforts in Ireland aimed at quality improvement are based mainly on the development of external accreditation. In addition, there are a considerable number of quality improvement initiatives being implemented at local level but efforts tend to lack central co-ordination. Examples of benchmarking to date are few but a number of hospitals recently (Brooks, 2000) took part in a benchmarking exercise of patient satisfaction on a voluntary basis. Work has also been undertaken on developing clinical audit.

This all suggests that, along with structural and organisational reforms, information will play a key role in management in Irish health services in the future: 'developing health information' was one of the frameworks for change identified by the 2001 *Health Strategy*. Information management systems will be required to enable data and information to be collected, analysed and disseminated across the range of health service areas and levels of the health system. At the same time, efforts will be required to ensure that decision makers use the data and information produced. We have outlined the range of concepts and measures of performance developed in the Irish health system and those used in other jurisdictions. Butler (2000) also suggests that, in order to get decision makers (e.g. managers, professionals, administrators) using the data produced, consideration needs to be given to the 'decision-usefulness' of data – the relevance, timeliness and accessibility of data to those who need it as a basis for decision making. Also, a management culture has to be created where data is valued as the basis for decisions and where managers, professionals and staff feel empowered to use it. Attention must be paid to the skills and competencies required to analyse, interpret and use the data effectively. The comparability and quality of measures and data must be such that decision makers have confidence in the data.

In Ireland, a National Health Information Strategy Committee is undertaking a comprehensive review of current arrangements for collecting, reporting and using health information, in order to develop a co-ordinated and integrated national health information system. The committee's vision is 'of information for health that is appropriate, comprehensive, high quality, available, accessible, and timely and that is used to enable and empower policy makers, managers, health professionals, patients, the community, and researchers to promote, protect, restore and maintain the health of individuals and the population' (NHISC, 2001). It was planned that a National Health Information Strategy would fall out of this work.

Another recent theme in health services reform is that health services should be better focused on improving health and social gain, addressing the causes of ill health, and the prevention and early detection of disease, over and above the treatment of symptoms. Inequalities in health within countries and regions is now as much a concern as inequalities between countries. So, although health status has improved considerably over recent years in Ireland, there is concern that Irish mortality rates are still comparatively poor and that there are significant differences in

This theme of stewardship is relevant to the discussion in Chapters 5 and 9 on the public-private mix and on the links between the state and the voluntary sector respectively. It also relates to the role of performance measurement (which was examined in Chapter 7) in enhancing accountability and permitting national oversight of the system as a whole.

From the perspective of the state, stewardship is a key theme in health care policy and the *World Health Report 2000* presented stewardship as a key role of government. From the perspective of private or voluntary organisations, clearly the key issues are the achievement of their goals or their response to the health care needs of their target population.

The public-private mix is a deeply important and controversial issue in Ireland at present. There is a growing political consensus that public patients should have access to acute hospital care which is comparable to that enjoyed by private patients. Comparative study suggests that inequities in access to acute hospital care between public and private patients are less significant in some other OECD countries than they are in Ireland.

On the other hand, as Chapter 5 indicated, most OECD countries have some form of public-private mix in health care, even if that mix has a somewhat different shape in each country.

In France, where inequities between public and private care are a less significant issue than in Ireland, general issues of health care funding and cost containment are nevertheless extremely challenging. A review of international experience suggests that while problems in the Irish health care system should not be minimised, they should be considered in the light of the significant funding and delivery challenges which other countries also face.

Finally, reflection on the comparative literature in both Chapters 5 and 9 stressed the need for clarity about the roles both of the state and of the private and voluntary sectors in the provision of health care. The achievement of such clarity is clearly not a simple or straightforward task but in Ireland, as elsewhere, debate on these issues will be enhanced by comparative reflection on developments in other countries.

References

Abel-Smith, B., Figueras, J., Holland, W., McKee, M., and Mossialos, E. (1995), *Choices in Health Policy: An Agenda for the European Union,* Luxembourg: Office for Official Publications of the European Community

ACPH (1994), *Strategies for Population Health: Investing in the Health of Canadians,* Prepared for a meeting of the Ministers for Health, Halifax, Nova Scotia, September 1994, Ottawa: Federal, Provincial and Territorial Advisory Committee on Population Health

ACPH (1996), *Report on the Health of Canadians,* Prepared for a meeting of the Ministers for Health, September 1996, Ottawa: Federal, Provincial and Territorial Advisory Committee on Population Health

Appleby, J. (1994), 'The Reformed National Health Service: A Commentary', *Social Policy and Administration,* Vol.28, No.4, pp. 345-358

Auditor General of Canada (1997), *Report of the Auditor General of Canada,* Ottawa: Office of the Auditor General

Australian Government Publishing Service (1996), *First national report on health sector performance indicators: public hospitals the state of play,* Canberra: Australian Government Publishing Service

Australian Productivity Commission (1997), *The Australian Private Health Insurance Review,* Canberra: Australian Productivity Commission

Banks, G. (1999), 'Australia's Industry Commission's Report on Private Health Insurance: Key Findings and Policy Recommendations', in Kinsella , R. and Ó Héalaí, R., *Private Medical Insurance and the Future of Irish Health Care,* Dublin: Oak Tree Press

Barrington, R. (1987), *Health, Medicine and Politics in Ireland 1900-1970,* Dublin: Institute of Public Administration

Bauld, L. and Judge, K. (1999), *Evaluating policies to tackle inequalities in health: the contribution of health action zones,* Paper presented to the European Health Forum, Gastein, Austria, October 6-9, 1999, PSSRU, University of Kent at Canterbury

Bégin, M. (1999), *The Future of Medicare: Recovering the Canada Health Act,* Ottawa: Canadian Centre for Policy Alternatives (http://www.policyalternatives.ca)

Bellanger, M. (1999), *The Effects of the Introduction of Market Forces into the Health System. France*, (Report for European Health Management Association, 1999) Dublin: EHMA

Benezval, M., Judge, K., and Whitehead, M. (1995), *Tackling Inequalities in Health: An Agenda for Action*, London: Kings Fund

Bocognano, A., Dumesnil, S., Frérot, L., Le Fur, P. and Sermet, C. (1999), *Santé, soins et protection sociale en 1998*, Paris: CREDES

Boyce, N., McNeil, J., Graves, D. and Dunt, D. (1997), *Quality and Outcome Indicators for Acute Healthcare Services: National Hospital Outcomes Program*, Canberra: Department of Health and Family Services, Australian Government Publishing Service

Boyle, R. (1999), *The management of cross-cutting issues*, CPMR Discussion Paper No. 8, Dublin: Institute of Public Administration

Brooks, A.M. (2000), *National Patients' Perception of the Quality of Healthcare Survey 2000*, Irish Society for Quality in Healthcare: Dublin

Buchan, H. (1998), 'Different countries, different cultures: convergent or divergent evolution for healthcare quality?' *Quality in Health Care*, Vol.7, (Suppl.), pp.S62-S67

BUPA (2000), *Irish Private Health Insurance and International Comparisons* (unpublished report), Dublin: BUPA Ireland

Busse, R. (1999), *The Effects of the Introduction of Market Forces into Health systems. National Report Germany*, Dublin: European Health Management Association

Busse, R. and Howorth, C. (1999), 'Cost containment in Germany: twenty years experience', in Mossialos, E. and Legrand, J. (eds), *Health care and cost containment in the European Union*, Aldershot: Ashgate

Busse, R. and Wismar, M. (1997), 'Health care reform in Germany: the end of cost-containment?' *Eurohealth*, Vol.3, No.2, pp.32-33

Busse, R., Howorth, C. and Schartwz, F. (1997), 'The future development of a rights based approach to health care in Germany: more rights or fewer?' in Lenaghan, J. (ed), *Hard Choices in Health Care – Rights and Rationing in Europe*, London: BMJ Publishing Group, pp.S21-47

Butler, M. (2000), *Performance measurement in the health sector*, CPMR Discussion Paper No.14, Dublin: IPA

Butler, M. (2002), *Evaluation in the Irish Health Services*, CPMR Discussion Paper, forthcoming, Dublin: IPA

Butler, M. and Boyle, R. (2000), *Service planning in the health sector*, CPMR Discussion Paper No.13, Dublin: IPA

Chief Medical Officer (1999), *Annual Report of the Chief Medical Officer*, Dublin: Department of Health and Children

Chief Medical Officer (2000), *The Health of our Children*, Annual Report from the Office of the Chief Medical Officer, Dublin: Department of Health and Children

CIHI (1998), *Navigating the Swirl: An overview of health informatics initiatives*, Ontario: Canadian Institute for Health Information

CIHI (1999), *Canadian Health Data Model: Draft*, Partnership for Health Informatics/ Telematics, Toronto:CIHI

CIHI (2000), *Health Care in Canada 2000: A First Annual Report*, http://www.cihi.ca

Cochrane, A. and Clarke, J. (ed 1993), *Comparing Welfare States. Britain in an International Context,* London: Sage

Colton, D. (1997), 'The Design of Evaluations for Continuous Quality Improvement', *Evaluation and the Health Professions*, Vol.20, No.3, pp.265-285

Comptroller and Auditor General (Amendment) Act, 1993. No.8 of 1993, Dublin: Stationery Office

Cousins, M. (1997), 'Ireland's Place in the Worlds of Welfare Capitalism', *Journal of European Social Policy*, Vol.7, No.3, pp.223-235

Currin, B. (1992), 'Summing up: civil society organisations in emerging democracies', Conference of Institute of International Education and Danish Centre for Human Rights on the Role of Voluntary Organisations in Emerging Democracies: Experience and Strategies in Eastern and Central Europe and in South Africa, Prague. Internet address: http://wn.apc.org/SAIE/civilxoc/

Dahlgren, G. and Whitehead, M. (1992), *Policies and strategies to promote equity in health*, Copenhagen: World Health Organisation Regional Office for Europe

Daniels, N., Kennedy, B. and Ichiro, K. (1998), 'Justice is good for our health', *Boston Review*, Vol. 25 No.1, February/March 2000

Deber, R., Narine, L., Baranek, P., ,Hilfer, N., Sharpe, N., Masanyk Duvalko, K., Zlotnik-Shaul, R., Coyte, P., Pink, G. and Williams, A. (February 1997) Summary of *The Public/Private Mix in Health care*, Paper commissioned by the

Canadian National Forum on Health, http://wwwnfh.hc-sc.gc.ca

Department of Health (1966), *The Health Services and their Further Development*, (White Paper) Dublin: Stationery Office

Department of Health (1986), *Health – the wider dimensions*, Dublin: Stationery Office

Department of Health (1989), *Working for patients*, London: HMSO

Department of Health (1994), *Shaping a Healthier Future: A Strategy for Effective Healthcare in the 1990s*, Dublin: Stationery Office

Department of Health (1995), *National Health Promotion Strategy 1995-2000*, Dublin: Department of Health

Department of Health (1996), *Cancer services in Ireland: A national strategy*, Dublin: Department of Health

Department of Health (1998), *Saving Lives: Our Healthier Nation*, London: HMSO

Department of Health (1999), *Reducing Health Inequalities: An Action Report*, London: HMSO

Department of Health and Children (1997), *Enhancing the Partnership: Report of the working group on the implementation of the health strategy in relation to persons with a mental handicap*, Dublin: Department of Health and Children

Department of Health and Children (1998a), *Working for health and well-being: Strategy Statement 1998-2001*, Dublin: Department of Health and Children

Department of Health and Children (1998b), *Report of the Advisory Group on Risk Equalisation*, Dublin: Department of Health and Children (unpublished report)

Department of Health and Children (1999a), *Building Healthier Hearts: The Report of the Cardiovascular Health Strategy Group*, Dublin: Department of Health and Children

Department of Health and Children (1999b), *Health Statistics*, Prepared by the Information Management Unit, Dublin: Department of Health and Children

Department of Health and Children (1999c), *White Paper on Private Health Insurance*, Dublin: Department of Health and Children

Department of Health and Children (2000a), *Minister Martin marks Millennium Budget with additional £1,000m expenditure for Health Services*, Press Release, 7 December 2000, Dublin: Department of Health and Children

Department of Health and Children (2000b), *National Health Promotion Strategy 2000-2005*, Dublin: Department of Health and Children

Department of Health and Children (2001a), *Quality and Fairness: A Health Strategy For You*, Dublin: Department of Health and Children

Department of Health and Children (2001b),*Primary Care: A New Direction*, Dublin: Department of Health and Children

Department of Health and Children (2001c), *Progress report on the Statement of Strategy*, Dublin: Department of Health and Children

Department of Health and Children (2001d), *Report of the Forum on Medical Manpower*, Dublin: Department of Health and Children

Department of Health and Children (2001e), *Report of the Forum on Medical Manpower/Report of the National Joint Steering Group on the Working Hours of Non-Consultant Hospital Doctors*, Dublin: Department of Health and Children

Department of Social Welfare (1997), *Supporting Voluntary Activity : a green paper on the community and voluntary sector and its relationship with the state*, (Green Paper) Dublin: Stationery Office

Department of Social, Community and Family Affairs (2000), *White Paper on a framework for supporting voluntary activity and for developing the relationship between the state and the community and voluntary sector,* Dublin: Stationery Office

Dixon, M. and Baker, A. (1996), *A Management Development Strategy for the Health and Personal Social Services in Ireland*, Dublin: Commissioned by the Department of Health and Children

Doherty, D. (1991), *More for Less: Providing Quality Services in Difficult Times*, Association of Health Boards in Ireland Conference – Working Together For Better Health: The Roles Of The Health Boards, Limerick, Conference paper

Donoghue, F. (1998), *Defining the nonprofit sector: Ireland*, Working Paper No.28, Dublin: National College of Ireland

Donoghue, F., Anheier H. and Salamon, L. (1999), *Uncovering the Nonprofit Sector in Ireland*, Dublin: National College of Ireland and Johns Hopkins University

Doyle, Y. and Bull, A. (2000), 'Role of private sector in United Kingdom', *British Medical Journal*, No.321, pp.563-565

Duriez, M. and Sandier, S. (1994), *The Health System in France,* Paris: CREDES and Ministère des Affaires Sociales

Durkan, J. (1998), 'The Market in Ireland for Healthcare Insurance', *Irish Banking Review*, Summer 1998, pp.53-62

EFQM (1999), *EFQM Benchmarking*, www.efqm.org/bmk/Bmk%20general.htm

Ellis, R. and Whittington, D. (1993), *Quality Assurance in Health Care: A Handbook*, London: Edward Arnold

Esping-Andersen, G. (1990), *The Three Worlds of Welfare Capitalism*, Oxford: Polity

European Commission (1997), E*uropean Economy, Reports and Studies, The Welfare State in Europe, Challenges and Reforms,* No.4, Brussels: Directorate-General for Economic and Financial Affairs

European Observatory on Health Care Systems (1999), *Health Care Systems in Transition*, United Kingdom. Copenhagen: European Observatory

Evans, J. and Ward, L. (ed), (1956), *The Social and Political Philosophy of Jacques Maritain*, London: Geoffrey Bles

Fairfield, G., Hunter, D., Mechanic, D. and Rosleff, F. (1997), 'Managed Care: Origins, Principles and Evolution', *British Medical Journal*, Vol.314, pp.1823-6

Fanning, B. (1999), 'The Mixed Economy of Welfare', in Kiely, G., O'Donnell, A., Kennedy, P. and Quin, S., *Irish Social Policy in Context*, Dublin: University College Dublin Press, pp.51-69

Faughnan, P. and Kelleher, P. (1993), *The Voluntary Sector and the State*, Dublin: CMRS

Field, M.G. (ed) (1989), *Success and Crisis in National Health Systems: A Comparative Approach*, Routledge: London

Fine Gael (2000), *Restoring Trust – a Health Plan for the Nation,* Dublin: Fine Gael www.finegael.ie

Finnis, J. (1980), *Natural Law and Natural Rights*, Oxford: Clarendon Press

Fitzgerald, A. and Lynch, F. (1998), 'Casemix measurement: assessing the impacts in Irish acute hospitals', *Administration* Vol.46, No.1, pp.29-54

FitzGerald, G. (2001), 'No one cried stop. A matter of decency…', http://www.irishhealth.com

Fleming, S. (2000), *From personnel management to HRM: key issues and challenges*, CPMR Discussion Paper No.16, Dublin: IPA

Folland, S., Goodman, A. and Stano, M. (1997), *The Economics of Healthcare*, London: Macmillan

Fox, J. and Benzeval, M. (1995), 'Perspectives on social variations in health', in Benezval, M., Judge, K., and Whitehead, M., *Tackling Inequalities in Health: An Agenda for Action*, London: King's Fund

Friel, S., MacGabhainn, S. and Kelleher, C. (1999), *The national health and lifestyle surveys: survey of lifestyle, attitudes and nutrition (SLAN) and the Irish health behaviour in school-aged children survey* (HBSC), Dublin: Health Promotion unit, Department of Health and Children; Galway: National University of Ireland, 1999

George, V. and Wilding, P. (1976), *Ideology and social welfare*, London: Routledge and Kegan Paul

General Medical Services (Payments) Board (2001), *Personal Communication*, Dublin: GMS Board

Ginzberg, E. (1999), 'The Uncertain Future of Managed Care', New England Journal of Medicine, (NEJM), Vol.340, pp.144-146

Gray, A. and Phillips, V. (1995), 'Recruitment and retention: what can the NHS learn from other employers?', *Health Services Management Research*, Vol.8, No.1, pp.38-46

Ham, C. (ed) (1997), *Health Care Reform, Learning from International Experience*, Buckingham: Open University Press

Harrison, M. and Calltorp, J. (2000), 'The reorientation of market-oriented reforms in Swedish health-care', *Health Policy*, Vol.50, pp.219-240

Hatcher, P. (1997), 'The health system of the United Kingdom', in Raffel, M., *Health care and reform in Industrialised Countries*, Pennsylvania: Pennsylvania State University

Hayes, T. (1999), *Perspectives on Funding in the Irish Voluntary Sector: Theory and Practice*, DCUBS Research Papers 1997-2000, No.37, Dublin: Dublin City University

Health (Amendment) Act (No.3) 1996, Number 32 of 1996, Dublin: Stationery Office

Health (Eastern Regional Health Authority) Act, 1999, Number 13 of 1999, Dublin: Stationery Office

Health Canada (1996), *Guide to project evaluation: a participatory approach*, Ottawa: Health Canada

Health Canada (1999), *An Inventory of Quality Initiatives in Canada: Executive Summary*, Ontario: Health Canada

Health Funding Authority (1999), *Briefing Papers to the Minister of Health,* Dunedin: Health Funding Authority

Hensey, B. (1988), *The Health Services of Ireland*, (4th edition), Dublin: Institute of Public Administration

Heidemann, E.G. (2000), 'Moving to global standards for accreditation processes: the ExPeRT Project in a larger context', *International Journal for Quality in Health Care*, Vol.12, No.3, pp.227-230

Higgins, J. (1981), *States of Welfare. Comparative Analysis in Social Policy*, Oxford: Basil Blackwell

Hochschild, J. (2000), T*he Principle of Subsidiarity and the Agrarian Ideal*, University of Notre Dame Department of Philosophy Online Papers, Indiana: University of Notre Dame, http://www.nd.edu/~ndphilo/papers/Subsidiarity.html

Home Office, Great Britain (1990), *Efficiency Scrutiny of Government Funding of the Voluntary Sector*, London: HMSO

Humphreys, P. and Worth-Butler, M. (1999), *Key human resource management issues in the Irish public service*, CPMR Discussion Paper No. 10, Dublin: Institute of Public Administration

Hupalo, P. and Herden, K. (1999), *Health policy and inequality*, Occasional Papers: New Series, No.5, Canberra: Commonwealth Department of Health and Aged Care

Iglehart, J. (1999a), 'The American Health Care System – Medicare', *New England Journal of Medicine*, Vol. 340, pp.327-332

Iglehart, J. (1999b), 'The American Health Care System – Medicaid', *New England Journal of Medicine*, Vol. 340, pp.403-408

ISO (2001), *ISO 9000 and ISO 14000 in plain language*, www.iso.ch/iso/en/iso9000-14000/tour/plain.html

Jaffro, G. (1996), 'The changing nature of Irish voluntary social service organisations', *International Journal of Public Sector Management*, Vol.9, No.7, pp.55-59

John Paul II (1991), *Centesimus Annus,* (Encyclical Letter), London: Catholic Truth Society

Johnson, N. (1987), *The Welfare State in Transition*, Brighton: Harvester Wheatsheaf

Joint Commission on Accreditation of Healthcare Organizations (JCAHO) (1999), Nation's three leading health care quality oversight bodies to coordinate measurement activities, http://www.obgyn.net/ENGLISH/PUBS/announcements/hcq_0520.htm

Jones, C. (1985), *Patterns of Social Policy: An introduction to Comparative Analysis*, London: Tavistock Publications

Kalisch, D.W., Aman, T. and Buchele, L.A. (1998), *Social and Health Policies in OECD Countries: A Survey of Current*

Programmes and Recent Developments, Labour Market and Social Policy Occasional Papers, No.33, Paris: OECD

Kinsella, R. (2001), 'Time to shift health burden from public sector', *Irish Times,* August 30, 2001

Kinsella, R. and Ó Héalai, R. (1999), *Private Medical Insurance and the Future of Irish Health Care,* Dublin: Oak Tree Press

Klein, R. (1998), 'Can Policy Drive Quality?', *Quality in Health Care,* Vol.7, (suppl.), pp.S51-S53

Labour Party (2000), *Curing our ills,* Policy document, Dublin: Labour Party

Le Grand, J., Mays, N. and Mulligan, J. A. (eds) (1998), *Learning from the NHS Internal Market: A Review of the Evidence,* London: King's Fund

Leahy, A. (1998a), 'Quality in the Irish Healthcare System', in McAuliffe, E. and Joyce, L. (1998) (eds), *Shaping a Healthier Future? Managing Healthcare in Ireland,* Dublin: Institute of Public Administration

Leahy, A. (1998b), 'Moving to a Quality Culture', in Leahy, A. and Wiley, M. (eds), *The Irish Health System in the 21st Century,* Dublin: Oak Tree Press

Leatherman, S. and Sutherland, K. (1998), 'Evolving quality in the new NHS: Policy, process and pragmatic considerations', *Quality in Health Care,* Vol.7, (Suppl.), pp.S54-S61

Leatt, P. and Williams, A.P. (1997), 'The Health Systems of Canada', in Raffel, M. (ed), *Health Care Reform in Industrialized Societies,* University Park: Pennsylvania State University Press, pp.1-28

Lebaube, A. (1999), 'L'économie sociale va-t-elle dissoudre dans le capitalisme?', *Le Monde Economie,* 28 September 1999, p.1.

LeGrand, J. (1982), *The Strategy of Equality: Redistribution of the Social Services,* London: Allen and Unwin

Levitt, R., Wall, A. and Appleby, J. (1995), *The Reorganised NHS (5th Edition),* London: Chapman and Hall

Light, D. (1998), 'Keeping Competition Fair for Health Insurance: How the Irish Beat Back Risk-Rated Policies', *American Journal of Public Health,* Vol. 88 No. 5, pp.745-748

Lomas, J. (1997), 'Devolved authority for health care in Canada's provinces. 4. Emerging Issues and Prospects', *Canadian Medical Association Journal* (CMAJ), Vol.156, No. 6, pp.817-823

Lomas, J., Woods, J. and Veenstra, G. (1997), 'Devolved authority for health care in Canada's provinces. 1. An introduction to the issues', *CMAJ,* Vol.156, No.3, pp.371-7

May, W. (1983), *The Physician's Covenant*, Philadelphia: Westminster Press

May, W. (1996), *Testing the Medical Covenant. Active Euthanasia and Health Care Reform*, Michigan/ Cambridge, UK: William B. Eerdmans Publishing Company

Mc Gauran, A. (2001), 'Handle with care', *Health Service Journal*, 18 January, 2001, pp.16-17

Mc Manus, L. (2000), *Statement accompanying Labour party document Curing our ills*, April 3, 2000

MCHPE (1999), *POPULIS : The population health Information System*, Manitoba: Manitoba Centre for Health Policy and Evaluation, University of Manitoba

Midland Health Board (1999), *Health Promoting Hospitals: Framework Document 1999-2002*, Midland Health Board

Ministère de l'Emploi et de la Solidarité (2001), *Conférence nationale de santé. Programme de santé présenté par Bernard Kouchner*, March 2001, Paris: Ministère de l'Emploi et de la Solidarité, http://www.emploi-solidarite.gouv.fr/index.asp

Ministry of Health (2000a), *New Jobs Reflect New Focus,* Ministry of Health, New Zealand, Media Release, 22 March 2000

Ministry of Health (2000b), *Ministry Leads Sector Change,* Ministry of Health, New Zealand Media Release, 6 April 2000, http://www.moh.govt.nz/change.html

Ministry of Health (2000c), *The New Zealand Health Strategy: Discussion Document,* Wellington: Ministry of Health

Ministry of Health (2000d), *Health Needs Assessment in New Zealand: An overview and guide*, Wellington: Ministry of Health

Ministry of Health (2001), *The New Zealand Public Health and Disability Act 2000,* News and Issues, Ministry of Health Website: http://www.moh.govt.nz

Moss, F. (1998), 'Quality in health care: getting to the heart of the matter', in Best, R. et al., *The Quest for Excellence: What is good health care?*, Kings Fund: London

Naylor, C. (1999), 'Health Care in Canada: Incrementalism Under Fiscal Duress', *Health Affairs*, Vol.18, No.3, pp.9-26

NCQA (1998), HEDIS 2000 List of Measures, http://www.ncqa.org/

NESC (1996), *Strategy into the 21st Century*, Dublin: Stationery Office

NESC (1999), *Opportunities, Challenges and Capacities for Choice,* Dublin: Stationery Office

NHISC (2001), *Our Vision and Objectives*, http://www.doh.ie/hstrat/nhis/visobj.html -

NHMBWG (1999), *Third national report on health sector performance indicators*, National Health Ministers' Benchmarking Working Group, Canberra: Commonwealth Department of Health and Aged Care

NHSE (1997), *NHS Priorities and Planning Guidance 1998/99*, EL (97) 39

NHSE (1997), *The new NHS. Modern. Dependable*, London: HMSO

NHSE (1998), *A First Class Service: Quality in the new NHS*, Government White Paper, London: HMSO

NHSE (1999), *The NHS Performance Assessment Framework*, Wetherby: Department of Health

NHSE (2000a), *The NHS Plan: A Plan for Investment, a Plan for Reform*, London: HMSO, http://www.nhs.uk/nhsplan

NHSE (2000b), *The New NHS. Modern. Dependable: Health Action Zones*, North West Regional Office: NHSE, http://www.doh.gov.uk/nwro/haz.htm

Nolan, B. and Wiley, M. (2000), *Private Practice in Irish Public Hospitals*, Dublin: Economic and Social Research Institute

O'Brien, J. (1994), *Healthcare Developments in the US*, Dublin; Institute of Public Administration (Discussion Paper of Health Services Resource Centre of IPA)

Ó Cinnéide, S. (1993), 'Ireland and the European Welfare State', *Policy and Politics*, Vol.21, No.2, pp.97-108

O'Connell, P. and Rottman, D. (1992), 'The Irish Welfare State in Comparative Perspective', in Goldthorpe, J. and Whelan, C. (eds), *The Development of Industrial Policy in Ireland*, Oxford: Oxford University Press

O'Donnell, A. (1999), 'Comparing Welfare States: Considering the Case of Ireland', in Kiely, G., O'Donnell, A., Kennedy, P. and Quin, S., *Irish Social Policy in Context*, Dublin: University College Dublin Press, pp.70-89

O'Ferrall, F. (2000), *Citizenship and Public Service: Voluntary and Statutory Relationships in Irish Healthcare*, Dundalk: Dundalgan Press Ltd

O'Hara, T. (1998), 'Current Structure of the Irish Health Care System – Setting the Context', in Leahy, A. and Wiley, M. (eds), *The Irish Health System in the 21st Century*, Dublin: Oak Tree Press

O'Sullivan, K. (2001), *States of Health*, *Irish Times*, October, 2001.

O'Sullivan, E. (1999-2000), 'Voluntary Agencies in Ireland – What Future Role?', *Administration*, Vol.47, No.4, pp.54-69

O'Sullivan, T. (1998), 'Changing Relationships and the Voluntary and Statutory Sectors', in McAuliffe, E. and Joyce, L. (eds), *A Healthier Future? Managing Healthcare in Ireland*, Dublin: Institute of Public Administration

Oakland, J.S. (1989), *Total Quality Management*, Oxford: Heinemann

OECD (1992), *The Reform of Health Care: A Comparative Analysis of Seven OECD Countries*, Health Policy Studies No.2, Paris: OECD

OECD (1995), *New Directions in Health Care Policy,* Health Policy Studies No.7, Paris: OECD

OECD (1996), *Health Care Reform: The Will to Change*, Health Policy Studies No.8, Paris: OECD

OECD (1997), *OECD Economic Surveys 1996-97 Ireland 1997*, Paris: OECD

Office of the Ombudsman (2001), *Report on Nursing Home Subventions*, Dublin: Office of the Ombudsman, http://www.irlgov.ie/ombudsman

Ovretveit, J. (1991), *Health Service Quality: An introduction to quality methods for health services,* Oxford: Blackwell Special Projects

Paton, C. (1995), 'Present Dangers and Future Threats: Some Perverse Incentives in the NHS Reforms', *British Medical Journal*, 1945, Vol.310, pp.1245-1248

Paton, C. (2000), *Scientific Evaluation of the Effects of the Introduction of Market Forces into Health Systems*, Dublin: European Health Management Association

Peillon, M. (1982), *Contemporary Irish Society: an Introduction,* Dublin: Gill and Macmillan

Pinker, R. (1992), 'Making sense of the mixed economy of welfare', *Social Policy and Administration*, Vol.26, No.4, pp.273-284

Poindron, P. (1997), 'Le malade, objet de tous les soins', Dossier No.363, http://www.galeriesociale.com/ese/html/dos363.html

Programme for Prosperity and Fairness (2000), Stationery Office: Dublin

Public Service Management Act, 1997. Number 27 of 1997, Stationery Office: Dublin

Quality Health New Zealand (2001), *HAPNZ: Health Accreditation Programme for New Zealand*, http://www. qualityhealth.org.nz/hapnz

WHO (1998a), *Highlights on Health in Ireland*, Copenhagen: WHO Regional Office for Europe

WHO (1998b), *The Solid Facts: Social determinants of health*, Copenhagen: WHO Regional Office for Europe

WHO (1998c), *Health 21 – health for all in the 21st century*, European Health for All Series No.5, Copenhagen: WHO Regional Office for Europe

WHO (1999), *Healthcare Systems in Transition*, United Kingdom, Copenhagen: WHO (European Observatory on Health Care Systems), http://www.observatory.dk/index-2.htm

WHO (2000), *The World Health Report 2000*, Health systems: improving performance, Geneva: World Health Organisation

Whyte, J. (1980), *Church and State in Modern Ireland*, Dublin: Gill and Macmillan

Wilding, P. (1992), 'Social Policy in the 1980s: An Essay on Academic Evolution', *Social Policy and Administration*, Vol. 26, No.2, pp.107-116

Wiley, M. (1994), 'Quality of Care and the Reform Agenda in the Acute Hospital Sector', in *Health: Quality and Choice*, Health Policy Studies No. 4, Paris: OECD

Wren, M.A. (2000), 'An Unhealthy State', *Irish Times*, October 2-6, 2001

Young, R. and Leese, B. (1999), 'Recruitment and retention of general practitioners in the UK: what are the problems and solutions?', *The British Journal of General Practice*, Vol. 49, pp.829-833

Current Issues in Irish Health Management

A Comparative Review